THE ESSENTIAL GUIDE TO FRANCHISING YOUR BUSINESS

A business owner's roadmap to franchise success

Roz Goldstein

Contents

About the Author

Roz Goldstein, Founder, Goldstein Legal

Roz Goldstein has extensive experience of franchising, having spent almost 20 years working in the industry for franchisor corporates before founding her own firm of solicitors, Goldstein Legal, in 2006.

Roz was elected to the British Franchise Association Board of Directors in 2016. She has obtained her Qualified Franchise Professional (QFP) qualification, and is a strong advocate of ethical franchising and franchise best practice. Roz can regularly be seen speaking at national franchise industry exhibitions and events.

Goldstein Legal provides specialist franchising and commercial legal services to businesses, and has been affiliated to the British Franchise Association since 2007. Full details about the firm are at: www.goldsteinlegal.co.uk.

HOW DOES FRANCHISING WORK?

Background

The 2015 bfa NatWest Franchise Survey demonstrates that the UK franchising industry is in rude health, contributing more than £15 billion to the UK economy as a whole. The sector continues to show growth year on year. There are currently more than 900 franchised systems in the UK, accounting for more than 40,000 franchisee-owned businesses, with more than 600,000 people employed in franchising.

The variety of different franchised businesses is astounding. From major consumer chains of coffee houses, food concepts and retail brands, through to business services in relation to training, recruitment, couriers and accountants. Whilst the number of retail franchised concepts has dropped in recent years, franchising in other sectors, such as hotels and catering, continues to grow strongly. The personal services sector has seen particularly strong growth. There are currently well over 200 different systems in the UK offering services such as domiciliary care, gyms, personal trainers, pet care and children's learning and entertainment.

Franchising experts point to significantly lower failure rates for franchisee-owned businesses, by comparison to SMEs in general. UK banks attribute this to the support provided by an established brand and a proven system of working, and therefore typically favour lending to franchised businesses over other stand-alone small businesses. 97% of franchisee-owned units in the UK reported profitability in 2015, with 56% saying that they are "quite" or "very" profitable.

More good news comes from the growth in British-owned concepts. Going back a couple of decades, a large proportion of franchised systems operating in the UK were imported from the US. Many of those brands are still here, and continue to go from strength to strength. But as at 2015, demonstrating how the UK franchising industry has matured, four out of every five franchised concepts operating here are UK based, and 38% of franchisors now export their franchised concept overseas.

But does all this mean that franchising is your guaranteed road to riches? Or that setting up and running a successful franchised concept is easy?

Unfortunately not. Beneath the compelling headlines about the strength of the UK franchising industry and the opportunities it presents, there are some substantial variables in terms of region, market sector and franchise profile. Not every business can be franchised successfully, and not every business-owner is cut out to be a franchisor. Franchising never works as a "get rich quick" scheme. It requires time, thought and money, all of which need to be invested for the long-term.

Importantly, no-one can deliver a franchise concept for you on a plate. No matter what anyone else might tell you, you will have to roll your sleeves up and put in some considerable hard work yourself. There are a number of excellent franchise advisors who are able to provide guidance and expertise to franchisors. But none of them will do it all for you.

This book sets out the key issues that you need to consider when deciding whether or not to franchise your business, and guidance on how to go about it. The book works around our user-friendly

Franchise Roadmap, which provides you with a transparent set of milestones on your route to franchising your business. We will refer to this Roadmap throughout this book.

What is franchising?

Although the term "franchise" can be used in a variety of contexts, in this book we are looking at franchising in terms of "business format" franchises. At its heart, the concept is fairly simple. In a business format franchise, an established business ("the franchisor") grants someone ("the franchisee") the right to trade under the franchisor's trade mark or trade name in a franchise agreement.

The franchisor develops a business concept, including a trade name and operating methods, and they train the franchisee in how to run their business using this concept. The franchisee operates their own business under the franchisor's name and under some fairly tight controls and guidance. These are set out in a franchise agreement and an operations manual. (We look at both of these in more detail in Step 4.) The franchisee has to operate the business in exactly the format specified.

The franchisor gives the franchisee the benefit of:

> ➢ a "business in a box" – in other words, a proven business model that the franchisee can run from day one, without having to invent it for themselves
> ➢ the strength, reputation and customer recognition of the franchisor's brand
> ➢ the essential (and unique) "know-how" of the business format, enshrined in an operations manual, and underpinned by a training programme
> ➢ ongoing business support.

In exchange, the franchisor receives:

- ➤ franchise fees from its franchisees – most typically an "Initial Fee" and ongoing royalties, commonly known as "management service fees"
- ➤ the potential for rapid business growth, through a network of franchisees
- ➤ increased brand recognition and reputation
- ➤ the opportunity of national and international brand expansion.

When it is done well, franchising presents a genuine "win-win" for both franchisor and franchisees, and this explains the overwhelming global success of franchising, in the UK and Internationally.

But as you will see as you read through this book, franchising is not for everybody. Nor is it a path to guaranteed riches with minimal or no effort. Launching a successful franchise requires a very specific set of skills and aptitudes. And it requires a potentially substantial investment of time, effort and money.

Types of franchise

Whilst the above is a very broad overview of how a franchise works, there are of course numerous variations, including:

Owner managed versus management franchises

A very large proportion of franchises are "owner managed", meaning that the franchisee buys the franchise and operates it themselves directly. The cost of acquiring the franchise is often modest, and the franchisee may well need a fair amount of support. Someone may, for example, buy a gardening franchise if they are a good gardener and they like working outdoors. But they may not be very comfortable creating spreadsheets, inputting data to a CRM system, or working out forecasts. As a franchisor, you will want to have systems that make that process easy for them.

On the other hand, with a management franchise, the franchise owner will employ a team of people to provide the goods or services to customers. They may have good management skills, but they may have little or no experience of the particular business sector that they are buying into.

Exclusive and non-exclusive territories

The majority of franchises are granted on an exclusive basis, meaning that the franchisee is given an exclusive territory, and the franchisor agrees not to allow anyone else to provide the relevant goods or services in that particular territory during the term.

But this does not apply to all franchises. There are a number (and this is most particularly in relation to business services) which do not have any exclusivity of territory.

Advantages of franchising

What are the advantages for the franchisor?

Franchising can give you a route to growing your business much more quickly and more effectively than growing your business organically. Here are some reasons why:

➢ Geographic growth

Let's say that you have successfully launched a restaurant concept in your home town.

To branch out from one outlet to three or four within, say, a 10 mile radius of the first one might be quite achievable. You can personally visit each site within a day, supplier deliveries are manageable, and it is most likely quite easy to shift staff from one site to another in line with customer flows at any one time.

But development on your own beyond this point can be difficult, without incurring the cost of a regional support team. And a regional support team may not pay for itself until you have a very much larger number of outlets, perhaps 20 or more.

With a franchise, you can appoint franchisees in hand-picked regions, who will develop the business for you. If you get it right - choosing the right franchisees in the right locations, and with a carefully planned training and support programme – your franchisees should be able to achieve the geographic growth of your brand that you can't manage on your own. Or, certainly, they can collectively get there much quicker than you can alone.

- ➤ Economies of scale

If well-planned, your franchise can give you substantial economies of scale, both in terms of the cost of products and equipment, and the cost of support.

It is no secret that quick service restaurant chains, such as MacDonalds, Burger King and KFC negotiate food costs that small operators can never hope to match. Likewise, some of the most successful service-based franchises are able to spread the cost of their support services, such as CRM systems and website functionality, across their whole franchised system, for the benefit of everyone.

- ➤ Low capital outlay and lower risk

Franchisees will incur the capital cost of development, rather than you. This is often a key driver in the decision made by retail concepts to grow through franchising, rather than organically. Hand-in-hand with this, therefore, is the fact that it is the franchisee, not the franchisor, who bears the risk of the success or failure of the franchise, and therefore the risk in the capital.

- ➤ Franchisee engagement

The franchisee will have incurred the capital cost of opening the franchise, including initial fees, set-up costs and fit-out costs, and has potentially taken on long-term financial commitments in the form of bank lending, leases etc. The franchisee is often therefore heavily invested in ensuring the success of their outlet, and this sometimes means that they have a greater sense of dedication and participation than an employee-manager would have.

➢ Franchisees know their territory

In the some of the most successful franchised systems, the franchisee benefits from their local knowledge and contacts. In the case of retail concepts, this may give the franchisee a sense of the best locations, and for service concepts, the franchisee can use his/her network to find customers and suppliers.

➢ National Accounts

Some franchise concepts benefit enormously from being able to service national accounts through their network of franchisees, securing some big customers who would otherwise be beyond their reach.

➢ Brand recognition

When it is done right, creating a network of franchisees increases the reach and awareness of your brand. This increased awareness helps you to secure customers, build value in your products/ service, and in turn this helps you to recruit more franchisees.

Advantages for franchisees – why would someone want to buy a franchise?

Your franchise proposition may be attractive to franchisees for a number of reasons:

➢ Proven business concept

Assuming that the franchisee makes a good choice when picking their franchise, the biggest advantage is that they are buying into an already established business concept. This should involve products and/or services that are well-developed, know-how that the franchisor has acquired over a period of years, and a brand that customers already recognise and value.

➢ Franchising resilience

Franchising continues to show substantial resilience, with the 2015 NatWest Franchising Survey showing that 90% or more of UK franchises have reported profitability, in all but one year since the start of the global recession in 2007/2008. The fact remains that new businesses operated under franchise are statistically far more likely to succeed than those that aren't. This gives franchisees a level of confidence about their new business that they would not have if they were setting up on their own. It likewise makes franchising, in many cases, a safer lending proposition to banks.

➢ Independence

Whilst the franchisee will be obliged to follow your operating methods exactly, and will often have minimum sales targets to achieve, they nevertheless have independence. They will own their own business, and this in itself can be a powerful attraction for individuals who simply want to be their own boss.

➤ Support

Although the franchisee will be "independent", they should have the benefit of ongoing support from their franchisor. They may also benefit through an exchange of ideas with other franchisees.

➤ Advertising and promotional spend

Many franchisors require their franchisees to contribute a small percentage of their sales towards a national advertising and marketing fund, managed by the franchisor for the benefit of the franchised network as a whole. This gives a franchisee the benefit of marketing campaigns that would be quite beyond the reach of a sole operator.

➤ Realisable value

When it goes well, the franchise enables the franchisee not just to earn a salary, but also potentially to realise a value in their business, by selling their franchise on at a later date.

A Franchise Roadmap

We will refer throughout this book to our Franchise Roadmap, which charts the tasks and considerations that lie ahead when you plan to launch a new franchise concept. The Roadmap sets out the process in four key stages:

STEP 1: Initial considerations

STEP 2: The Franchise Development Plan

STEP 3: Defining the Franchise Proposition

STEP 4: Implementation

FRANCHISE ROADMAP

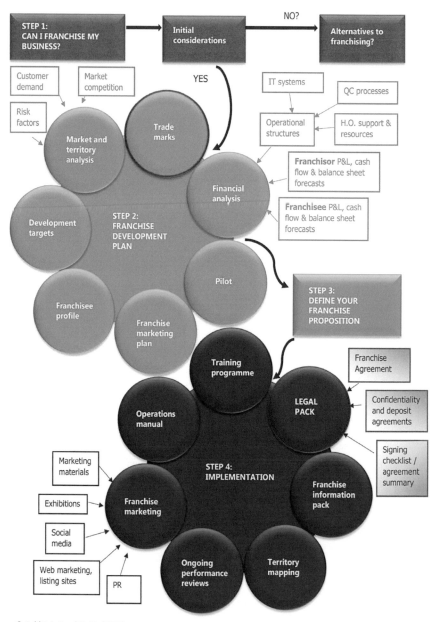

STEP 1: CAN I FRANCHISE MY BUSINESS? → **Initial considerations** → NO? → **Alternatives to franchising?**

YES

- Customer demand
- Market competition
- Risk factors

Market and territory analysis

Trade marks

STEP 2: FRANCHISE DEVELOPMENT PLAN

- Development targets
- Franchisee profile
- Franchise marketing plan
- Pilot

Financial analysis

- IT systems
- QC processes
- Operational structures
- H.O. support & resources
- **Franchisor** P&L, cash flow & balance sheet forecasts
- **Franchisee** P&L, cash flow & balance sheet forecasts

STEP 3: DEFINE YOUR FRANCHISE PROPOSITION

STEP 4: IMPLEMENTATION

- Training programme
- Operations manual
- **LEGAL PACK**
  - Franchise Agreement
  - Confidentiality and deposit agreements
  - Signing checklist / agreement summary
- Franchise information pack
- Territory mapping
- Ongoing performance reviews
- **Franchise marketing**
  - Marketing materials
  - Exhibitions
  - Social media
  - Web marketing, listing sites
  - PR

© Goldstein Legal Limited 2016

14

STEP ONE: SHOULD YOU FRANCHISE YOUR BUSINESS?

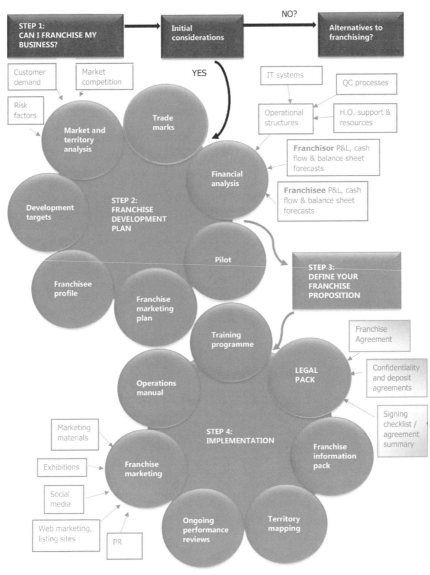

FRANCHISE ROADMAP

STEP 1: CAN I FRANCHISE MY BUSINESS? → Initial considerations → NO? → Alternatives to franchising?

YES

Customer demand
Market competition
Risk factors

Market and territory analysis
Trade marks

IT systems
QC processes
Operational structures
H.O. support & resources

Franchisor P&L, cash flow & balance sheet forecasts

Financial analysis

Franchisee P&L, cash flow & balance sheet forecasts

Development targets

STEP 2: FRANCHISE DEVELOPMENT PLAN

Pilot

STEP 3: DEFINE YOUR FRANCHISE PROPOSITION

Franchisee profile

Franchise marketing plan

Training programme

Franchise Agreement

LEGAL PACK

Confidentiality and deposit agreements

Operations manual

Signing checklist / agreement summary

Marketing materials
Exhibitions
Social media
Web marketing, listing sites
PR

STEP 4: IMPLEMENTATION

Franchise marketing

Ongoing performance reviews

Territory mapping

Franchise information pack

© Goldstein Legal Limited 2016

Bear in mind that almost anyone in business can create a franchise. The challenge is creating a successful one. Not everyone succeeds at that, and many people who attempt it and fail would have been better off not attempting it at all. It is relatively easy to design some franchise marketing materials, create something that looks like an operations manual, and get someone to draft some legal documentation. Armed with not much more than this, many new franchisors will go on to invest substantial sums in glossy marketing materials, exhibition stands and franchise recruitment websites, in the hope and expectation that willing franchisees will appear before their eyes, cheque-books in hand, and that riches will undoubtodly flow. The blunt truth, however, is that this will not happen. If anyone promises you otherwise, do not believe them.

Not only will riches not flow into your pockets this way, but all manner of additional troubles will present themselves:

> Even if you have cut corners on costs all the way along, by the point you realise that your franchise concept is going to fail, you will inevitably have sunk fair amount of cash into things that are now no use to you.
> As well as dealing with your own disappointment, you may have a collection of fairly disgruntled franchisees, unhappy that your promises to them have come to nothing.
> These franchisees might be tempted to sue you.
> You may have a financial exposure to investors or lenders who have backed you.
> You have damaged your business reputation, making it hard to start over with any credibility.

In Step 2 we will look at the importance and value of thorough business planning. But before we even get to the planning stage, your Step 1 needs to be a measured and objective review of whether franchising is going to work for you, and whether there are any better alternatives.

Getting good advice at Step 1 is critical, and we discuss this further below. Here are some of the key things that you and your advisers will want to think about before you embark on a franchising plan.

Is your business replicable?

When you grant a franchise, you are essentially licensing a third party to run a replica version of your business. Often, but not always, in a different geographical location to yours. It therefore has to be possible for a franchisee (with suitable training) to copy your business model successfully. Many business concepts are replicable, but not all are. You will potentially find it difficult if your business:

- depends on a specific customer base that few franchisees would have access to
- depends on a limited region or location
- is heavily reliant on one person's personality or attributes
- is dependent on a rare or specific skill set, such that it is difficult to train other people, or where the pool of potential suitable franchisees is extremely narrow or specialised.

Is there an established demand for products and services of the type you provide?

Someone has to be first to market for every new product or service, and if it is you, you may be lucky and succeed in making a lot of money from it. But it is near to impossible to launch a franchise in respect of anything which isn't already tried and tested. If you are confident that your product is going to be the next big thing, then you need to run it as a pilot first. (We will look at pilot operations in Step 2.) Preferably, you need to franchise something for which there is already a proven customer demand, even if you are nevertheless confident that your products or services will be of a better quality, or better value, than anyone else's.

What "know-how" do you have?

There is unfortunately a rather fine line between being replicable, and being simply generic. This is regrettably where a number of franchisors fail. Notwithstanding that you need an established demand for your product or service, there has to be something special about your particular, so that it requires your "know-how" to make an ongoing success of it.

The term "know-how" covers a multitude of things. It is all the special techniques that you have developed for the operation of your business and that make it successful. It includes confidential and often unique elements.

In franchising, there ideally needs to be two elements of "know-how":

- the knowledge that will be shared with your franchisees as part of your initial training programme; and
- the ongoing service, support and/or technologies that the franchisor goes on providing to its franchisees throughout the life of their franchise.

Some franchised systems will fail because there is none (or not enough) of the second element above. We will look at this in more detail in Step 2.

What brand recognition do you have?

At its heart, a franchise agreement is a licence granted by the owner of a brand name to allow another person to use that brand name in connection with their business. The strength of that brand name, its recognition and reputation by its customer base and the public in general, will have a material impact on the potential of your franchise concept. Brands with little or no visibility are going to be very difficult to market to potential franchisees.

Developing a franchise network is a great way of building your brand reputation. But if your concept isn't already well-known, at least within your pool of potential customers, you will have some hurdles to overcome. Having a strongly recognisable brand for your business is not necessary on day one of your franchising project, but the foundations of it should be there before you start. You should, at the very least, have a brand name which is registrable as a trade mark in your main operating country, and should be working with your lawyer or trade mark agent on getting it registered. You should also have secured your relevant domain names. (We will look at this in more depth in Step 2.)

Finally, you will want a suitable budget set aside for PR and brand-awareness, so that you can be building customer recognition whilst you develop your franchise concept.

Will franchising suit you and your business?

Just because you *can* franchise your business, doesn't automatically mean you *should*. Franchising is not for everyone. You will need the stamina and patience to create your franchise operation. Profits may come in the long term, but in the short term they certainly will not. In the planning stage of your franchise project, and in the first year or more of implementation, you will spend substantially more on your system than you receive in revenue from your franchisees. Do not go into franchising if your motivation is immediate cashflow.

You will need working capital for the franchise set-up. Whether you self-fund, or whether you take on investors or lenders, you will need to do some prudent budgeting. (We deal with this in Step 2.)

A bit of honest self-reflection can be valuable before you embark on franchising, particularly in terms of what gives you satisfaction at work, and what motivates you on a personal level. Let's assume, for a moment, that you are a tree surgeon. The things that you enjoy in your daily life might be the outdoors, the fresh air, being your own boss, and being answerable to no-one but your clients. From the point that you launch your tree surgeon franchise, things change. You will spend more time in an office, sending emails and working on Excel spreadsheets, and although you are still technically your own boss, you now have a community of franchisees who and have expectations of you and require daily support. If this is not a life you would enjoy, you would be better off staying a tree-surgeon, and looking at other ways of growing your business or increasing your revenues.

Although it is difficult to generalise, here are some personal attributes that can be helpful for a franchisor:

> High level of organisational skills
> Process-driven
> Comfortable with delegating
> Good interpersonal and communication skills
> Good at gaining consensus

Some character traits which will be a challenge in franchising are:

> Poor organisational skills
> Not good at planning
> No head for (or interest in) figures
> Frequently change your mind about things
> Impatience or short-temper
> Not a "people person".
>

If the above sounds even a little bit like you, franchising is very likely not the best route forward for your business.

One of the easiest and most common mistakes that people make in franchising is to launch their concept too soon. It is understandable that, fired-up with passion for your brand and business concept, and once attracted to the idea of franchising, you can find yourself jumping rather too quickly.

Your key driver for franchising should be that your own careful analysis that it is the best thing for your business. Not that someone else has offered to take on a franchise of your business, when otherwise you wouldn't have thought of it. There is, of course, nothing wrong with responding to an offer that is presented to you. And some now extremely successful franchises have come about that way. But franchising is a long process. It is not by any means a guaranteed road to riches, and involves business risk. It is unlikely to generate profits for you in the first couple of years (or longer). In fact, during the initial stages, it is likely to involve a substantial investment of time and money on your part, with no immediate return.

You will not be able to fund your franchising project out of the first couple of franchises that you launch. You will need to have funded it up front, with the resources to carry most of the cost until your franchise development is well underway.

The level of success of a franchise is very largely dictated by how much thought and preparation you put into it at the beginning. Realistically, if your franchise was slightly rushed or ill-considered when you launched it, it is unlikely that the wrinkles will smooth themselves out later.

Mark Scott is Director, Franchise Development in the **NatWest & RBS Franchise Team**

Mark has many years of experience advising and lending to franchised businesses. Mark says that the keys to a successful franchise are *"Having sufficient resources, including people. And a good brand reputation, developed through the franchisor's existing business.*

Most franchise concepts will also need some sort of unique selling point (or USP)" says Mark. *"KFC have their fabled secret recipe, for example. You need to have something that gives you an edge over your competitors.*

There are some business sectors which are strong in franchising – food concepts are a particularly good example. A well-run coffee shop or fast food concept, with a well-known brand, is likely to operate with margins that are sufficient to allow for a reasonable management service fee, and the turnover would most likely be high enough to ensure that both the franchisee and the franchisor earn a decent return."

Mark sees a bright future ahead for the UK franchising sector: "We see continued growth for franchising in the future, both in terms of numbers of franchise concepts and total numbers of franchisees. Where established franchisors are concerned, Mark says: *"Franchise system failures are rare, and tend not to occur unless the market in which the franchise concept operates has changed, and the franchisor is unable to keep up with it."*

The later chapters in this book set out some of the key steps to franchising. But let's look first at some initial considerations, before you even start your first step.

Is your business mature enough?

There is no hard and fast rule here. But as a general guide, you should ideally ensure that you have a good couple of years of successful trading behind you before you think about franchising. Remember that your franchisees are paying for your business format, so it needs a tangible value. At the very least you want to have developed that format to the point where you can prove that the concept works and that it makes money. It is going to be difficult to convince anyone of that before you have some obvious track record of profitability, and some basis for believing in the longevity of the concept. After all, your franchisees are likely to be signing up to a franchise term of perhaps 3 to 5 years. You need to be able to demonstrate to them convincingly that, although it may take several months or longer to break even, they will make a good return over the lifetime of their franchise.

All of the above is much easier to demonstrate if you have a strong set of cash-flow, profit & loss and balance sheet statements of your own.

Alternatives to franchising

You won't know if franchising is the perfect route for growing your business, unless you have considered what your alternatives are. So do not proceed with a franchising project before you consider whether anything else would work better for you.

Here are some of the most common alternatives to franchising:

> Organic growth

The Introduction sets out what the advantages are of franchising over growing your business yourself. But achieving your own organic growth can be very effective for a number of businesses.

It is a better choice for anyone who wants complete control over their relationship with their clients or customers, as franchising by definition involves relinquishing much or all of that to your franchisees.

Organic growth can often be appropriate where there is no geography, or regional limits, around the products or services you provide. Internet-based businesses tend not to lend themselves to franchising, unless there is some element of locality to the service that franchisees are well-placed to fulfil.

Here are some of the most common alternatives to franchising:

> Brand licensing

Franchising and licensing are very similar. In fact, both of them are a form of licence to use a trade mark in connection with a business. Just as with a franchise, there is a brand owner (in this case a Licensor) who grants another entity (a Licensee) the right to use the Licensor's brand name and/or other intellectual property rights in connection with businesses carried on by the Licensee. As with a franchise, the licensee's business benefits from the brand and intellectual property of the licensor, and the licensee pays fees to the licensor accordingly.

The important difference is that a licence arrangement tends not to involve the replication of an existing business format. In many cases, the intention is the exact opposite, with the licensor licensing their brand to a third party who will be able to exploit it in a consumer sector in which the licensor has no presence or expertise. The perfume industry is a good illustration - the majority of all the big name fragrances are in fact made and sold by just two or three big perfume houses. "Calvin Klein", "Cerruti", "Vera Wang", "Chloe" and "Lagerfeld", for example, are all are manufactured and distributed by Coty under licence from the brand owners. And the revenues that the likes of Disney, Warner Brothers and BBC Worldwide derive from merchandise licensing in many cases exceed the profits from the relevant film or TV rights.

Licensing also works well where the licensor has developed some specific technology, know-how, brand images or designs, which are attractive to licensees who wish to incorporate it into their existing businesses. Take software and database technology, for example, which are invariably exploited through licensing.

A licence can be easier to manage than a franchise. As a general rule, a licence arrangement is cheaper and easier to set up than a franchise concept, and less demanding in terms of your on-going management time.

The licensee has more freedom to run their business their own way, and they often add the licence to their existing business as a means of expanding the scope of products or services that they provide. For example, there are also a number of businesses who have developed unique coaching and personal development tools which they then licence to training establishments who provide the licensed products alongside other products.

Similar to a franchise, a licence agreement has to focus

carefully on quality assurance and compliance with the licensor's standards. Products or services sold under licence should enhance and complement the reputation of the licensor, and the licence agreement must allow the licensor to "pull the plug" whenever quality or compliance are compromised.

> ➤ Distribution

If your business is all about selling products, and your key objective is to grow your sales channels, then distribution might be worth considering rather than franchising. Car dealerships and IT suppliers are typical examples. Distributor arrangements work well where branding is not an important element of the product, or where the branding is someone else's, eg you are a wholesaler of a well-known brand. In a distributor arrangement, you sell your products to a distributor, and he/she then sells them on to a third party. The distributor owns the relationship with their end customer. There are significant limits on your ability to control who they sell to, and you cannot control or limit the price at which the products are sold.

> ➤ Agency

The key difference between an agency and a distributor arrangement is that if you appoint an agent, they are selling products on your behalf. This is different to a distributor, who is technically selling on their own behalf. The agent may find the customer, but it is you who enters into the contract with that customer. You can control your own pricing, but you are also liable entirely for any defects in the products or services supplied.

Note that there are some specific UK and European laws

that affect agency arrangements. Most particularly, these entitle agents in many cases to significant damages on termination of an agency arrangement. Details about that are beyond the scope of this book, but suffice to say that you should not appoint an agent to sell goods on your behalf without seeking legal advice first.

Choosing the right advisors

There is no secret magic to franchising. As franchise professionals, none of us is in possession of unique secrets which hold the key to franchising success. As with all other forms of business creation and development, no consultant or expert can waive a magic wand, and conjure up a business for you that will give you guaranteed riches. You should avoid at all cost anyone who tells you that they can. The success (or otherwise) of your business is going to depend on you – your determination, hard work and confidence – and your ability to come up with, and develop, a good idea.

If you pick the right consultant, he or she can be invaluable. However, their value comes from utilising the benefit of their experience to steer you in the right direction, acting as a sounding board, challenging your assumptions, analysing your market potential, and helping you to structure a plan. In addition, they will have a wealth of knowledge of other franchise operators, and they will be well-connected with other advisors who can provide additional support where you need it. But they will never be able to create the entire franchise concept for you successfully and hand it to you on a plate. It will involve a lot of time, effort and engagement on your part, as well as cost. It is unwise to embark on any franchising project unless you fully have the appetite for this.

Before you even contemplate engaging a professional adviser, it is well worth making good use of the free information and guidance which is publicly available on the British Franchise Association's (bfa's) website: **www.thebfa.org**. The bfa have a wealth of useful background information about the principles of franchising, and the do's and don'ts of running a successful franchised system. Read this first before you choose an external adviser. It may well inform your decision.

It is clear even from a cursory glance online, that there are a myriad of advisors, consultants and experts offering to help you franchise your business. Many of them have excellent credentials, but your choice is going to be a largely personal one, and so it pays to shop around. Here are some tips of the things to consider:

➢ British Franchise Association affiliation

It would be almost certainly be risky and unwise to launch a franchise in the UK without having the input and guidance of at least one professional who is an affiliate of the bfa. The bfa are selective about who they appoint as affiliates. They expect the advisers to have knowledge and experience and a successful track record in franchising. They also expect their members to adhere to the Code of Ethics. This Code, and the bfa's guide to it, are available from **www.thebfa.org**. Whilst bfa affiliation can never in itself be an absolute guarantee, it does at least indicate some minimum standards.

You may decide in time that you want your franchise to become a member of the bfa. Using a bfa affiliate in your franchise project should ensure that your business is steered in the right direction for this to become possible if you want it. If you use advisors who are not bfa affiliates, you will find yourself having to duplicate time and cost when you later decide that you want to join the bfa.

Make sure therefore that you have at least one professional adviser in your team, whether it is a franchise lawyer, accountant or consultant, who has bfa affiliation.

> If it sounds too good to be true……

…… *it probably is.* We have all heard this before, and it is as relevant in choosing franchise advisors as it is for anything else.

If anyone promises that they will *"do 90% of the work for you and find you franchisees"*, or anything along those lines, you should be highly sceptical.

Be similarly wary of anyone who offers you a do-it-yourself style package for a couple of thousand pounds, or a "complete" package for not very much more. No bfa affiliate would operate this way. You will waste time and money with this, and will very likely need to start all over again when you find out that the package was - to say the least - not quite what was promised.

> Scope of services and costs

Ideally, choose a consultant who will tailor their service around your particular needs. Be wary of a "one size fits all" approach. No two businesses are identical, and likewise no two franchise development projects are the same either.

A good franchise consultant will be able to provide you with an outline of an action plan, broken down into stages of activity, and a timeline. Step 2 gives you a broad idea of the elements to expect. The plan should also set out stages of cost, so that you can manage your budget.

It should be possible for you to look at the outline plan with your consultant, to work out what elements you need them to do for you, what elements you can do together, and what elements you can do yourself. The advisor should be able to adjust the scope of services, to allow for any particular resources that you may already have available, and your individual skill set.

Make sure that you are paying for what you need, and that you are not tied-in to paying for a suite of products or services, whether you need them or not.

- ➤ Personality

Your choice of advisor is going to be based as much on personality fit as on anything else. You will need to be able to work closely together. So take the time to talk to a few advisors before you decide who will be best for you.

- ➤ Track-record in my business sector?

This can be useful. But the opposite can also sometimes apply. Having an adviser cast a critical eye over your business, with no pre-conceptions at all about how that particular type of business ought to work, can sometimes be insightful.

- ➤ References/testimonials

It is always worthwhile following up on references and testimonials. Ideally, getting permission to speak directly to one or two of that advisor's previous or existing clients, to get a feel for how the relationship worked.

How much will it cost you to launch your franchise?

There are many different variables that impact on your budget, so there really is no standard answer to this question. But chances are that if a new franchise concept fails before it has got off the ground, then this is, more likely than not, down to the franchisor under-budgeting. A lack of adequate investment is the single biggest cause of new franchise failures. Launching a successful new franchise concept requires an investment of money, as well as time and energy. It cannot be done on a micro-budget, and if anyone tells you otherwise, they are misleading you.

Many successful franchisors will have spent upwards of £30,000 to launch a new franchise concept in the UK, and some considerably more. This will include expenditure on brand marketing and PR, as well as more specifically on franchise recruitment marketing. Franchising is a competitive business. As a franchisor, you will be competing hard against other concepts for franchise recruitment. Many of them will have spent sizeable sums on brand promotion. It is unrealistic to assume that you can rival their success without doing likewise. Trust your instincts and be wary of anyone who offers to franchise your business for you for a few thousand pounds. They are highly unlikely to make a success of it, and you risk making a costly mistake.

Bear in mind that if you plan your franchise development well, particularly with focus on the financial analysis described in Step 2, you should have a robust plan for ensuring that, over a period of time, your costs of setting up your concept are recouped from your franchisees.

You will be in a better position to budget for your franchise development once you have completed Steps 2 and 3, and you will see that we look at a number of variable cost elements in those sections of this book. Some particular factors that will have a specific impact on the cost of your franchise development include:

> How much of the preparation and implementation will you do yourself? Do you have the necessary skills within your own organisation to put together some or all of your own franchise development plan? Even if you have the skills, do you have the manpower to manage this on top of the day to day running of your existing business?

> In light of that, what external consultancy support will you need, and what will be the scope (and cost) of that support?

> What systems will you need to run your franchise? If you do not already have a sophisticated CRM system for your business, it is likely you are going to need to get one. Without it, you will have insufficient visibility of your franchisees' businesses, and the time you spend trying to manage your franchisees (and their customers) will likely make you wish you had never started a franchise in the first place.

> Where will you find your franchisees? Even if you already have one or two potentially interested candidates, you are very unlikely to be able to build a robust network of franchisees for the long-term without a chunky budget for franchise marketing and promotion. There are various different routes open to you for franchise recruitment,

and your choice will depend on your specific business. But whichever route(s) you choose, there will be upfront costs.

STEP TWO – FRANCHISE DEVELOPMENT PLAN

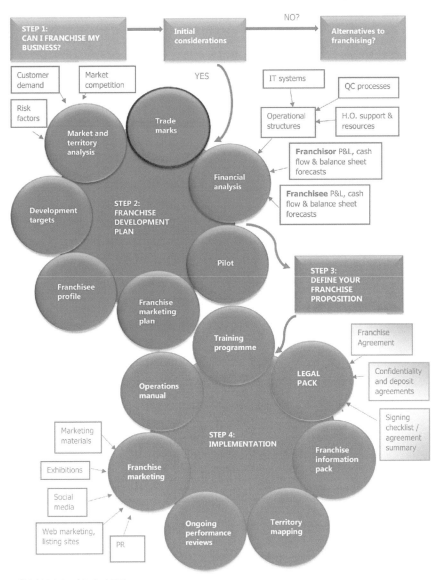

FRANCHISE ROADMAP

STEP 1: CAN I FRANCHISE MY BUSINESS?

Initial considerations

NO?

Alternatives to franchising?

Customer demand

Market competition

YES

Risk factors

IT systems

QC processes

Operational structures

H.O. support & resources

Market and territory analysis

Trade marks

Financial analysis

Franchisor P&L, cash flow & balance sheet forecasts

Development targets

STEP 2: FRANCHISE DEVELOPMENT PLAN

Franchisee P&L, cash flow & balance sheet forecasts

Pilot

STEP 3: DEFINE YOUR FRANCHISE PROPOSITION

Franchisee profile

Franchise marketing plan

Training programme

Franchise Agreement

Operations manual

LEGAL PACK

Confidentiality and deposit agreements

Marketing materials

STEP 4: IMPLEMENTATION

Signing checklist / agreement summary

Exhibitions

Franchise marketing

Franchise information pack

Social media

Web marketing, listing sites

PR

Ongoing performance reviews

Territory mapping

We all know the saying *"Fail to Plan – Plan to Fail"*. This is as true with franchising as with anything else. So often franchise development fails because the franchisor fails to think the details through and as a result falters at an unforeseen hurdle. Just as likely, the franchisor runs out of funds for the necessary work, not having budgeted realistically at the outset.

It may go by various titles – Franchise Development Plan, Feasibility Study, Evaluation Analysis – but whatever you choose to call it, your plan needs to be your analysis of your franchising opportunity, and your blueprint for achieving it. Once you have completed your plan, you should have a very clear idea of how you are going to create your franchise, who will need to do what, over what timescales, how much you will need to invest, how quickly you and your franchisees can expect to make a return on your and their investment.

Furthermore, a well-planned and well thought-out Franchise Development Plan will determine your Franchise Proposition, which is at the heart of your franchise.

Should you run a "pilot operation" first?

The purpose of a pilot franchise is to test out your franchise concept, by running a separate business which replicates as much as possible the way that a franchisee will operate. The importance of a pilot is underlined by the bfa in their guide to the Code of Ethics, which stresses that you should *"have operated a business concept with success, for a reasonable time and in at least one pilot unit"* before starting your franchise network.

The benefits are obvious, in that once you have a pilot which has been running for a year or two, you have a concrete illustration of the way the franchises will work. You can test the time that it takes to set the franchise up, what it costs you in terms of training, initial support, ongoing support, and any specific services that you are providing (eg systems). At the same time you can assess how easily a franchisee can gain customers and a sufficient level of turnover, and therefore how long it will take him or her to achieve a return on their investment.

The pilot gives you the opportunity to test and improve your operations manual, with the benefit of experience. Likewise, it gives you a chance to test out your assumptions about your criteria for choosing your franchisees. If there are particular skills or aptitudes that your franchisees need to have in order to succeed, it is best you work this out before you have signed your first five or six, rather than afterward.

The pilot will help to establish some brand recognition. And if you are setting up a retail concept, it will enable you to trial one or more different types store layouts, décor and facia etc.

Ideally, you will run one or more pilot operations before you launch your franchise concept fully, and certainly before you embark on full-scale franchise recruitment initiatives. The learning you will gain from your pilot will enable you to fine-tune your franchise proposition, give you strong data on which to base any sales projections, and will enable you to get your franchise marketing materials, your franchise proposition and support plans into good shape before you invest substantial sums in marketing your franchise.

Having a well-run pilot with a successful track record can be an enormous boost to franchisee recruitment, and protects you to some degree against the risk of claims by franchisees for mis-selling, or misrepresentation.

But of course, all of the above depends on the quality of the pilot. For example, proof that a pilot food concept has worked well in a shopping mall food court in Lincoln is not much of an indicator that the same concept will work in a high street location in Reading. So to cover all bases, you would need to run a number of pilots in different types of location. Recruiting suitable pilot operators to do this, and then managing them all, may not be hugely practical for you.

In reality, it can also be difficult to run any pilot on a truly arm's length basis. Often, the pilot franchisee is a relation or a business partner of the person developing the franchise concept. You may spend longer supporting them and setting them up than you actually account for (meaning that your estimate of franchisee profitability in the early years is potentially unrealistic). They may already have knowledge of the business, and/or customer connections, which means that it is easier for them to get up and running than it would be for a truly independent, and newly recruited, franchisee. Building your franchise sales projections around your pilot without making a suitable allowance for these things can be positively dangerous.

It is possible to treat your first one or two recruited franchisees as pilots, by giving them preferential fee rates, in exchange for making it clear to them that your system is still in development and may therefore require adjustment during the term of the franchise. But the problem with this approach is that you are recruiting your first one or two franchisees somewhat in the dark. You may be taking them on without knowing precisely what skills or attributes they need, or how much support you will need to provide them. You will also be a bit limited in your ability to market the franchise in the early stages, as you will not be able to provide objective cash-flow forecasts etc.

The sensible approach, when setting up a pilot, is to be as objective as you can about the costs of it. Keep it as arm's length as you possibly can, and err on the side of caution in assessing its performance, taking care to make allowances where necessary. In all cases, plan your franchise recruitment to allow for a pause after the first one or two appointments, so that you can track their performance over a reasonable period of time, and make adjustments to you franchise proposition, your fee structure, operations manual and franchisee recruitment criteria before you invest substantial sums in franchise shows, glossy brochures and other recruitment initiatives.

Financial Analysis

By far and away, this is the most important piece of planning and analysis that you need to do before you embark on your franchising project. There is a world of difference between launching a franchise – which almost anyone can do, and running a successful and profitable one – which lots of businesses attempt and fail at.

You may have an excellent product offering, you may have cornered a specific new market, and you may have the most genuine intentions for your franchisees to share in your success. But all of this can come to nothing without methodical and objective financial planning. This may sound dull, but it is the absence of objective forecasting that is the prime culprit for franchisor failures.

Here are some of the issues that make the difference between a successful franchise system, and an unsuccessful one:

> Under-capitalisation. New franchisors can all too easily under-estimate what it is realistically going to cost them to set the franchise up. What they do spend on the project comes to nothing when they run out of funds and have to abandon the project.
> "Over-selling". One of the most common traps that franchisors fall into is over-promising and under-delivering. This is often genuinely unintentional. Without prudent, reality-based financial forecasts, based on real data (rather than guess-work or aspiration) franchisors sometimes let their enthusiasm for their concept run away with them. The result can be litigation, and/or the complete collapse of the franchise.

- The franchisor assumes that the Initial Fees will be cash in their pocket, having over-looked the full cost of training and setting up each new franchisee.
- The franchisor makes no profit. In their eagerness to put together a business model that enables franchisees to make a good return, new franchisors all too often underestimate how much time, effort and overhead they will need to put into managing their franchisees. Unless you are embarking on a charitable, or "not-for-profit", business model, it is unwise to start any new franchise unless you have solid grounds for forecasting that you will make a return on your hard-work and investment.

Although possibly not the most creative or exciting element of your franchising project, your Financial Analysis is almost certainly the most critical to your ongoing success.

Even if you have the skills, time and resources to do much of your franchise planning yourself, this is one area where you are likely to want external, expert advice.

As you can see from the Franchise Roadmap, there are a number of different elements that feed into the Financial Analysis. You will not be able to complete your Franchise Development Plan, and define your Franchise Proposition, until you know things like:

- What level of turnover and net profit can your franchisees realistically expect to make, and over what period?
- How much is it going to cost you to launch the franchise and support your franchisees? How long will it take you, and how many franchisees will you have to recruit, in order to recoup your initial investment?

➤ What should you charge your franchisee, in terms of initial fees, ongoing management service fees, and other service fees, eg for training, systems licences etc.

Here are the main things that you will want to think about:

Setting up your franchise model – costs and timeline

➤ You need to budget for your total outlay of capital on your franchise set-up, including any consultancy and legal fees, trade mark registration costs, PR and branding, and all other up-front costs.

➤ Allowing for the fact that, whilst setting up your franchise concept, you are also most likely running your existing business at the same time, how long is it going to take you until you are ready to launch your concept? And now long will it take you to recruit your first franchisee?

➤ How many franchisees will you have to recruit before you recoup these upfront outgoings, and how long is that going to take you? How therefore will you fund your set-up costs in the meantime?

Operating Structures and Head Office support

➢ What systems and resources will your franchisees need to run their businesses? What will be the roles and responsibilities of franchisor and franchisee?

➢ To what extent will the franchisees rely on ongoing support from you? What form will that support take?

➢ Will you have regular meetings with each franchisee? At what intervals?

➢ What initial and on-going training will you provide?

➢ Will you review your franchisees' performance annually, and agree their business plan for the next coming year?

➢ Will you organise franchisee meetings? What budget have you set for this?

➢ What resources will you need to support your franchise network, in the short, medium and long term?

➢ Will you need additional staff? Whether for handling telephone calls from customers or franchisees, making site visits to franchisees, or supporting franchisees through their set-up process?

➢ How will your franchisees deliver products or services to their customers?

➢ To what extent will you control the supply chain? Will the franchisee be dependent on supplies from you? Or will they use approved or nominated suppliers? Is the supply chain sufficiently robust to support a growing franchise system? If you retain a margin or mark-up on the supply of products, will the franchisees still benefit from a competitive pricing structure?

IT Systems

- Will you need new systems, eg for customer relationship management (CRM)? Will the cost of this be scalable, so that you pay for it incrementally as your franchisee base increases? Or will it require some substantial up-front investment on your part?
- Who will provide maintenance and support for the systems? How much will that cost?
- If IT systems or support are provided by a third party, will you be charging each franchisee for the cost of this? Will that cost be built into the franchise fee, or charged as a separate?
- Who will be maintaining your website? Do you have internal resources to set up a webpage for each new franchisee, or will you have to out-source it at a cost?
- Likewise, who will establish email addresses for franchisees, and provide ongoing IT maintenance and support?
- Will you keep ownership and control of a central customer telephone line? Will you keep ownership of individual franchisee telephone numbers?

Quality Control (QC)

- How will you monitor the performance and standards of your franchisees? What resources will you need for this? Bear in mind that this will become an increasingly burdensome task the more franchisees you recruit and the wider their geographical spread.
-

Profit & Loss, Cash Flow and Balance Sheet Projections

You will want to have two sets of projections – one for your franchisees and one for you as franchisor. Each set should ideally cover Years 1 to 5, or at least Years 1 to 3.

You will feed into your projections the key elements of your operational structure that you have budgeted for, along the lines set out above. Your next task is to add forecasts of your franchisees' sales, and forecasts of your revenue from franchisees, into your projections. The result should provide you with as much comfort as possible that both you, and your franchisees, can run profitable businesses.

Your projections will have to include some initial assessments of:

- ➢ What you will provide your franchisees by way of a Start-Up Package
- ➢ How much you will charge for an Initial Fee
- ➢ What ongoing fees you will charge your franchisees

However, you may well adjust these when you finalise your Franchise Proposition, and you should therefore be prepared to do a few iterations of your projections, with different assumptions on fees, so that you can determine what will work best for you. Your projections are not set in a tablet of stone. They will be evolving documents that you will work on as your project develops - improving, correcting and fine-tuning them before you launch your franchise and start recruiting franchisees.

There is simply no substitute for getting these forecasts done to a professional standard before you launch your franchise. If figures are not your "thing", it is worth paying someone else to do it for you. In any event, an independent third party will have an objectivity that you will not.

What is a balance sheet?

This draws on information from your Profit & Loss, and shows the value of the assets and liabilities in your organisation at a precise point in time (eg at the end of each year). Lenders, creditors and investors will look for your balance sheet forecasts to show a strong level of "Net Worth" – in other words, they will want to see that your assets are worth more than your liabilities. They may also look for your forecasted "gearing ratio" – how your Net Worth compares with your borrowings.

An example of a simple form of forecast balance sheet can be found overleaf.

BALANCE SHEET END YEAR 1

FIXED ASSETS

CAPITALISED EXPENDITURE		34,000
LESS DEPRECIATION	20%	6,800
TOTAL		27,200

CURRENT ASSETS

STOCK	2,000	
BANK	27,485	
DEBTORS	14,000	
TOTAL		43,485

CURRENT LIABILITIES

VAT	4,573	
OTHER		
TOTAL		4,573

NET CURRENT ASSETS	38,912
TOTAL ASSETS	66,112

LONG TERM LIABILITIES

BANK LOAN	31,556	
OTHER		
TOTAL		31,556

TOTAL ASSETS LESS LIABILITIES	34,556

CAPITAL

OWNERS INVESTMENT	30,000
P & L Yr 1	4,556
P & L Yr 2	
TOTAL	34,556

What is a Profit & Loss Account?

A forecast P&L will show you whether you are likely to make a profit or loss over a specific period of time. It will show a gross profit – being total sales less cost of sales. It will also show a Net Profit, which is what is left after you have deducted your expected overheads from your Gross Profit.

Your "EBITDA" is your Earnings (ie net profit) before Interest, Tax, Depreciation and Amortisation.

Example — PROFIT AND LOSS ACCOUNT — YEAR 1

		M1	M2	M3	M4	M5	M6	M7	M8	M9	M10	M11	M12	TOTAL
SALES		8,000	9,000	10,000	11,000	12,000	13,000	14,000	14,000	14,000	14,000	14,000	14,000	147,000
COST OF SALES	30%	2,400	2,700	3,000	3,300	3,600	3,900	4,200	4,200	4,200	4,200	4,200	4,200	44,100
GROSS PROFIT		5,600	6,300	7,000	7,700	8,400	9,100	9,800	9,800	9,800	9,800	9,800	9,800	102,900
FRANCHISE FEES	6%	480	540	600	660	720	780	840	840	840	840	840	840	8,820
RENT & RATES		1,333	1,333	1,333	1,333	1,333	1,333	1,333	1,333	1,333	1,333	1,333	1,333	15,996
UTILITIES		150	150	150	150	150	150	150	150	150	150	150	150	1,800
VEHICLE COSTS		100	100	100	100	100	100	100	100	100	100	100	100	1,200
OWN DRAWINGS		1,600	1,600	1,600	1,600	1,600	1,600	1,600	1,600	1,600	1,600	1,600	1,600	19,200
STAFF COSTS		1,316	1,316	1,316	1,316	1,316	1,316	1,316	1,316	1,316	1,316	1,316	1,316	15,792
MARKETING		1,000	500	100	100	100	100	100	100	100	100	100	100	2,500
PROFESSIONAL		200											600	800
ADMIN COSTS		60	60	60	60	60	60	60	60	60	60	60	60	720
TELEPHONE		75	75	75	75	75	75	75	75	75	75	75	75	900
MAINTENANCE		50	50	50	50	50	50	50	50	50	50	50	50	600
INSURANCE		100	100	100	100	100	100	100	100	100	100	100	100	1,200
BANK LOAN INTEREST		192	192	192	192	192	192	189	185	182	178	174	171	2,231
VAT LOAN INTEREST		-	-	-	-	-	-	-	-	-	-	-	-	-
XEROX LEASING		770	770	770	770	770	770	770	770	770	770	770	770	9,240
OTHER LEASING		2,260	753	753	753	753	753	753	753	753	753	753	753	10,543
TOTAL OVERHEADS		9,686	7,539	7,199	7,259	7,319	7,379	7,436	7,432	7,429	7,425	7,421	8,018	91,542
NET PROFIT (b/f dep & tax)		-4,086	-1,239	-199	441	1,081	1,721	2,364	2,368	2,371	2,375	2,379	1,782	11,358
DEPRECIATION		567	567	567	567	567	567	567	567	567	567	567	567	6,804
NET PROFIT (b/f tax)		-4,653	-1,806	-766	-126	514	1,154	1,798	1,801	1,805	1,808	1,812	1,215	4,556

Cashflow Forecasts

Your P&L projections will forecast profitability. The cashflow forecast, on the other hand, shows you whether from one month to the next you have enough cash to pay your bills. If you don't, your business will fail, even if it is technically "profitable" on paper.

Every business should therefore have a cashflow forecast, kept up to date each month. It might literally make the difference between "make" or "break".

Here is a typical example of a cashflow forecast. You will see that it projects what your bank account (or your franchisee's bank acoount) is expected to look like at the end of each month.

It shows figures for each month from months 1 to 12, and to the right are cumulative figures for the whole of "Year 1".

CASHFLOW FORECAST END YEAR 1

	%	M-1	M1	M2	M3	M4	M5	M6	M7	M8	M9	M10	M11	M12	TOTAL
CAPITAL		30,000													30,000
BANK LOAN		35,500													35,500
SALES RECD IN MC	0%		-	-	-	-	-	-	-	-	-	-	-	-	
SALES RECD IN 30	100%		-	8,000	9,000	10000	11000	12000	13000	14000	14000	14000	14000	14,000	133,000
TOTAL SALES EXC VAT			-	8,000	9,000	10,000	11,000	12,000	13,000	14,000	14,000	14,000	14,000	14,000	133,000
VAT OUTPUT	20%			1,600	1,800	2,000	2,200	2,400	2,600	2,800	2,800	2,800	2,800	2,800	26,600
TOTAL SALES INC VAT				9,600	10,800	12,000	13,200	14,400	15,600	16,800	16,800	16,800	16,800	16,800	159,600
TOTAL INCOME		65,500	-	9,600	10,800	12,000	13,200	14,400	15,600	16,800	16,800	16,800	16,800	16,800	225,100
COST OF SALES			2,400	2,700	3,000	3,300	3,600	3,900	4,200	4,200	4,200	4,200	4,200	4,200	44,100
FRANCHISE FEES			480	540	600	660	720	780	840	840	840	840	840	840	8,820
RENT & RATES			1,333	1,333	1,333	1,333	1,333	1,333	1,333	1,333	1,333	1,333	1,333	1,333	15,996
UTILITIES			150	150	150	150	150	150	150	150	150	150	150	150	1,800
VEHICLE COSTS			100	100	100	100	100	100	100	100	100	100	100	100	1,200
OWN DRAWINGS			1,600	1,600	1,600	1,600	1,600	1,600	1,600	1,600	1,600	1,600	1,600	1,600	19,200
STAFF COSTS			1,316	1,316	1,316	1,316	1,316	1,316	1,316	1,316	1,316	1,316	1,316	1,316	15,792
MARKETING			1,000	500	100	100	100	100	100	100	100	100	100	100	2,500
PROFESSIONAL			200	-	-	-	-	-	-	-	-	-	-	600	800
ADMIN COSTS			60	60	60	60	60	60	60	60	60	60	60	60	720
TELEPHONE			75	75	75	75	75	75	75	75	75	75	75	75	900
MAINTENANCE			50	50	50	50	50	50	50	50	50	50	50	50	600
INSURANCE			100	100	100	100	100	100	100	100	100	100	100	100	1,200
START UP STOCK		2,000													2,000
CAPITAL EXPENDITURE		34,000													34,000
BANK LOAN INTEREST					577			577			556			523	2,233
XEROX LEASING			770	770	770	770	770	770	770	770	770	770	770		9,240
BANK LOAN REPAYMENTS									657	657	657	657	657	657	3,942
OTHER LEASING			2,260	753	753	753	753	753	753	753	753	753	753	753	10,543
VAT INPUT	20%	6,800	1,325	956	948	1,020	1,092	1,164	1,236	1,236	1,236	1,236	1,236	1,356	20,841
VAT DUE							-6,628		3,325			4,493			1,190
TOTAL EXPENDITURE		42,800	13,219	11,003	11,532	4,759	11,819	12,828	16,665	13,340	13,896	17,833	13,340	14,583	197,617
C/F BANK BALANCE		-	22700	9481	8078	7,347	14589	15870	17,542	16,477	19,937	22,842	21,809	25,269	
TOTAL INCOME		65,500 -		9,600	10,800	12,000	13,200	14,400	15,600	16,800	16,800	16,800	16,800	16,800	
TOTAL EXPENDITURE		42,800	13219	11,003	11,531	4,758	11,819	12,827	16,665	13,340	13,896	17,833	13,340	14,583	
CLOSING BANK BALANCE		6,800	2260	1,709	1,701	8,401	1,845	1,917	-1,336	1,989	1,989	-2,504	1,989	2,109	27,486

Why is the difference between *"cash"* and *"profit"* so important for your business?

Chris Roberts, Franchise Finance

Chris Roberts is a director of Franchise Finance Limited, an independent franchise finance consultancy and training company. Their services include arranging finance (bank and leasing), the preparation of business plans, and providing training courses and workshops.

This is what Chris had to say about the important difference between "profit" – what you see on your P&L forecast; and "cash" – what your cash flow forecast will show.

"People like talking about "Profits". How much they are going to make or how much they have already made. Yes this is hugely important because you don't want to be running a loss making business. However, what is even more important is the answer to the question "Do you have enough cash to pay your bills, as and when they become due"? A simple fact is that businesses go bust when they run out of money.

Let's assume a franchise supplies goods on 30 days credit and on a Friday afternoon they make a £20,000 sale for goods they bought for £10,000. They despatch the goods and raise an invoice. Therefore they can legitimately claim to have made a "profit", and they may therefore decide to celebrate that weekend with several bottles of wine! However, if they come back into work on the Monday morning and need to pay the VAT bill or perhaps the wages and they don't have enough cash in the bank to do so, they are in big trouble. Yes they have made a "profit", but it is having sufficient amount of cash, or working capital that really matters. So remember:

TURNOVER IS VANITY *** PROFIT IS SANITY *** CASH IS REALITY"

Market Analysis

Customer demand

It is dangerous to launch any new business (franchised or otherwise) without having some hard data that there is a proven demand for your product or service, and that customer demand, and the prices that customers are willing to pay, will be sufficient to sustain a business.

You will want to consider:

> - What data can you gather about the size and value of the market for your products or services? Is the market growing, and will it continue to do so?
> - Who will be your customers, and your franchisees' customers? Are they limited by socio-economic factors, age, gender or geography?

If you have run a pilot operation for a year or more prior to planning your franchise, you should already have some strong market data. But be wary about local demographic factors. It does not follow that consumer appetite will be consistent throughout the UK. You may therefore need to do some sort of market research, or pay someone else to do it.

If you have not yet run a pilot operation, you need to take a cautious approach here. Your first franchisee will effectively be your "pilot", and you should not be recruiting him or her purely on the grounds of your guesswork and aspiration.

Market competition

You will want to think about:

> ➢ Who your competitors are?
> ➢ How will you match or beat your competitors on price, quality or customer service?

Also consider how easy (or difficult) it is for another competitor to enter your market and replicate your product or service. Is there sufficient customer demand for you to be able to withstand this?

Risk Factors

It is prudent to identify at an early stage if there are risks, sensitivities or contingencies around the potential success of your franchise. If these issues are significant, it might mean that franchising is simply not appropriate for you at this time. Otherwise, you can explore, and hopefully resolve, these as your project develops.

Typical risk factors can include the following:

> ➢ The business takes advantage of a particular consumer trend that may not stay the distance. "Fads" will come and go. If your system is rooted in one speciality, whether it is a food concept, or dance classes, or a specialised fitness programmes, you will run into difficulty with your model when that particular speciality wanes in popularity. This risk is manageable so long as you have sufficient flexibility in your operational model, and franchisees with sufficient skills, to adapt to changes in trends.

- The business offers technology solutions that are at risk of becoming obsolete over time. Again, your system needs to have some scope to adapt, and your franchisees will need to have sufficient breadth of skills.
- The business is seasonal. Will there be sufficient demand to keep franchisees engaged and motivated during quieter times of year?
- Your "pool" of potential franchisees with the requisite skills and experience is limited, putting inevitable limitations around your franchise development plans.
- The business lacks uniqueness, or is easy to copy, with the result that your market may become saturated with competitors
- The business relies on government grants or is in a sector which is (or might in future be) regulated, and is therefore at risk of changes in government policy.

How do you protect your brand? Trade Marks and Intellectual Property

Trade Marks

The foundation of any franchise system is a trade mark licence. As a franchisor, you are granting a franchisee the right to trade under your brand name, and your brand name is essentially a trade mark. You are well advised, therefore, to ensure that your trade mark is registered. You can only market your franchise in good faith if you have taken steps first to register and protect your trade mark. If you haven't done so before you start, your franchising project will be on shaky grounds. Not only would you be misleading your franchisees as to the strength and value of what they are paying for, but your whole system will be at risk of a lawsuit if someone claims to have prior rights to the name you are using.

It is easy to fall unwittingly into a trap here. You could be forgiven for concluding, having registered your business name as a limited company at Companies House, and having secured your domain names, that your brand is safely protected and that you are the legal owner of it. Unfortunately, this is not the case. Generally speaking, a registered trade mark will take precedence over a domain name. If someone else got to the Intellectual Property Office before you did, your entire franchise concept might falter. The time, energy, thought and cost that you put into choosing a brand name and logo for your business will all be jeopardised if it turns out that someone else had already registered a word or logo which is the same or similar to yours, and which is in the same or a similar category of goods or services.

Some brief explanation of how trade marks work:

Typically, trade marks are either "word marks" or "figurative marks". A word mark, as the name suggests, protects the word or words. Some well-known examples would be "Marks & Spencer", "Pepsi Cola", and "Jaguar".

"Figurative marks" (or "logos") protect a figurative image, or an image combined with a word. Some famous examples would be

(These marks are registered trade marks of Porsche and BP, respectively)

A word mark generally affords the strongest form of trade mark protection, as they prevent third parties from using the word (or words), or anything similar, no matter how they appear, and regardless of how they are stylised.

Figurative marks protect the imagery of the logo. This can be very valuable. But they do not protect the *name* of your brand. This is one reason why companies with valuable brand names will each tend to have a sizeable portfolio of trade marks, encompassing both word marks and figurative marks. (And note that they will spend many millions of pounds every year protecting, updating and defending that portfolio.)

Another important point to note about trade marks is that they are registered by reference to a category or categories of goods and services. Some examples: furniture is in class 20, and clothing is in class 25. Beauty-care services are in class 44. Cleaning services are in class 37.

For your trade mark to remain protected in any category, you need to be using it in that category. If you don't, then eventually your mark will become vulnerable to revocation for non-use. This is why it will almost never be possible to protect your mark for everything. At your franchise planning stage, you will want to make a sensible assessment of which categories of goods and services you are going to be supplying, at least in the short to medium term.

An additional pressure comes from the sheer volume of trade marks – words and logos – that are already registered and that continue to be applied for. There might be an infinite number of potential images, but there is a finite number of words in the English language. A word mark will generally get you stronger protection than a logo. European Union trade marks (EUTMs) give the owner trade mark protection throughout EU member states. And then there are marks registered under the "Madrid Protocol", which give the owners prior rights across (currently) 97 countries. The chances are quite high that if you haven't already registered a trade mark, your chosen brand name will already be taken by someone else, somewhere in the world.

It therefore makes sense to invest in your trade mark protection right at the early stage of your franchising project, and certainly before you fall deeply in love with your branding. Specialist legal advice is essential here. Trade mark protection can be tricky and expensive, and your legal adviser should be able to ensure that your money is spent protecting you in the most cost-effective and advantageous way.

Other forms of Intellectual Property

Your trade mark is a critical element of your franchise. But there are other forms of intellectual property that will matter to you as well. Some key examples are:

> **Copyright.** In the UK, copyright exists automatically, without any requirements for you to register it, in "original works". These would potentially include your marketing materials, your operations manual, your training materials, and the wording, images and designs included in them. Copyright lasts for a set period, usually the life of the author plus 70 years from the end of the calendar year of their death. If something has copyright, any unauthorised copying would amount to a copyright infringement, and may even constitute a criminal offence. The details of copyright law and other intellectual property rights are outside the scope of this book, so you must seek the advice of an expert. At the very least, you must take steps to record who and when has created any copyright works for you, and you should ensure that your materials contain a suitable copyright notice, such as a © followed by the name of copyright owner, and the year of publication.

> **Database rights.** There will potentially be database rights in your CRM system, your website, and various other systems. A database could be a hugely valuable asset in your business, and you will want to have robust procedures in place to protect it, particularly as it is likely to be accessible by your franchisees.

➤ **Design rights.** These protect the appearance of a product, or part of it, and can be registered or unregistered.

➤ **Confidential Information.** You have a right to protect your confidential information, and this could include things like know-how and trade secrets which are a key part of your business format.

You need to know what intellectual property your business has, and then take sensible steps to protect it. There is no substitute to taking advice from a legal professional in this regard.

Territory Plan

Key to your Franchise Development Plan will be an assessment of how many franchisees you are going to recruit, in what locations, and in what timescales.

Most franchises are location-based, with each franchisee operating within a defined "Territory". Usually, but not always, these Territories are granted to each franchisee on an exclusive basis, and the franchisor commits not to operate in the franchisee's territory, or grant anyone else the right to do so.

As most franchise opportunities are marketed to franchisees on the basis that they come with an exclusive territory, your franchisees are likely to be nervous if you are offering a system without exclusivity. They will be concerned that you might flood their area with other franchisees, or sell directly to customers in their area yourself.

Having said this, there are a number of highly successful franchise concepts which do not have territory exclusivity. This more often occurs in franchise systems which provide B2B (business-to-business) services, such as training, business consultancy, freight services. It is less common in businesses that sell to consumers. But note that there are a number of coffee chains and quick service restaurant concepts that do not give their franchisees exclusive territories.

We will come on to Territory Mapping in more detail at Step 3. But at Step 2, for the purposes of your Franchise Development Plan, you will want to have a preliminary idea as to

➢ how you will carve out each territory
➢ what demographic features each territory needs to have

➢ which part or parts of the country you will focus on, and in what order.

This is not least because you need to plan your own internal resources, and have a sufficient budget for any external support or advice. You will need more staff, and substantially more time, to recruit, say, 20 franchisees all over the country in your first 18 months, than you will if you are focussing on, say, 7 to 8 in that period, all in the Home Counties. The time and cost involved in this needs to be factored into your Franchise Development Plan.

Your initial territory plans may well change as your franchising project develops. But nevertheless, some initial territory analysis as part of Step 2 will help you to make a reasoned assessment of how many franchises you will open, and therefore how much revenue you will receive from Initial Fees, in each of your first few years.

Franchisee Profile

It is true that when you get to the Implementation stage (Step 3), you are likely to finesse your thinking on franchisee profiles. It will be key to how you choose to market your franchise. But some consideration of this at the planning stage is important too. At a minimum, it worthwhile evaluating what skills, experience or attributes your franchisees are going to need to possess. Drawing from the well-known saying *"Recruit for attitude, train for skills"*, you will want to think about what attributes you can teach, as part of your initial training programme, as opposed to the capacities or experience that prospective franchisees need before you can even consider them.

Of course, the franchised systems that have the least difficulty recruiting franchisees will tend to be the ones with fewer barriers to entry – in other words

- ➢ where the required level of cash investment from the franchisee is low, and
- ➢ where the franchisor is able to train the franchisee in all the required skills and know-how.

Conversely, you will have a steeper mountain to climb if your franchisees have to have certain professional experience or qualification before they start, and/or where the set-up cost is substantial.

The profile that will be the most appropriate for your franchisees is going to vary widely from one franchise to another, and from one business sector to another. A hairdressing franchise may well require its franchisees to have prior experience and/or qualifications in hair styling. A management consultancy franchise may need its franchisees to have prior business experience at a relatively senior level. On the other hand, if you are setting up a cleaning franchise, where each franchisee will be a manager of their own staff, your franchisee does not need to know how to clean. But he or she might need to have experience of recruiting, managing and motivating people. Accurate profiling is clearly easier when your business is well developed. Some of the more established franchise systems have been able to tailor their franchisee profile and recruitment criteria over a period of many years, to the point that recruitment decisions are highly systemised and objective. But for a new franchisor, franchisee selection criteria will unavoidably have an element of guess-work to them. You will almost inevitably make mistakes in the early stages, but you should be able to learn from them.

As part of the planning stage, therefore, it is worth giving some thought to things like:

> whether there are particular skills or experience which your franchisees will need to have in advance
> what skills you can teach during their Initial Training
> whether there are particular levels of physical fitness required
> how much capital they need to have at their disposal

This will give you an idea as to the level of challenge that that lies ahead when you start your recruitment, and you can feed this into your Franchise Development Plan.

The most well-established franchisors will have franchisee recruitment criteria that have been established with great care over a period of time. It is a mark of some of the most successful and ethical franchise systems that they communicate their criteria openly and clearly, and that they do not deviate from those criteria, no matter how tempting it might be.

Expense Reduction Analysts (ERA) have been running for many years. Here is an example (reproduced by kind permission of ERA) of how they communicate their franchisee criteria:

Characteristics Of Potential Franchisees

wants to be self employed not cant get a job

a good attitude and core skills

self motivated & enthusiastic

the ability to speak to people

Expense Reduction Analysts

Teachable – Training, don't want "know it all" types

The ability to fund the franchise fee £39,900 + VAT

12 months working capital & living expenses
(Banks will lend up to 70% of the total capital required)

Franchise Marketing Plan

There are a number of different channels open to franchisors to market their opportunity to prospective franchisees. Your choices for franchise recruitment will have detailed focus when you get to Implementation at Step 3. Nonetheless, you need to have a suitable budget for this, factored into your Financial Analysis for your Franchise Development Plan at Step 2.

Recruiting enough of the right type of franchisees is, for many franchisors, their single biggest challenge. Do not assume that, from the moment you launch your franchise, you will have a stream of suitable franchise applicants at your door. As a general rule, there are more franchise opportunities on the market, than there are prospects who want to take them. So it would be dangerous to underestimate the cost involved. Franchise marketing and recruitment may well be your biggest item of expenditure, not just in the initial launch phase, but on a continuing basis.

STEP 3: DEFINING YOUR FRANCHISE PROPOSITION –

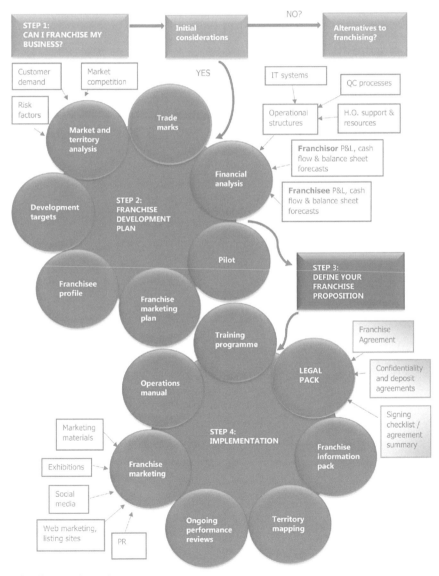

FRANCHISE ROADMAP

STEP 1:
CAN I FRANCHISE MY
BUSINESS?

Initial
considerations

NO?

Alternatives to
franchising?

Customer
demand

Market
competition

YES

IT systems

QC processes

Risk
factors

Trade
marks

Operational
structures

H.O. support &
resources

Market and
territory
analysis

Financial
analysis

Franchisor P&L, cash
flow & balance sheet
forecasts

Development
targets

STEP 2:
FRANCHISE
DEVELOPMENT
PLAN

Franchisee P&L, cash
flow & balance sheet
forecasts

Pilot

STEP 3:
DEFINE YOUR
FRANCHISE
PROPOSITION

Franchisee
profile

Franchise
marketing
plan

Franchise
Agreement

Training
programme

LEGAL
PACK

Confidentiality
and deposit
agreements

Operations
manual

Signing
checklist /
agreement
summary

Marketing
materials

STEP 4:
IMPLEMENTATION

Franchise
information
pack

Exhibitions

Franchise
marketing

Social
media

Web marketing,
listing sites

PR

Ongoing
performance
reviews

Territory
mapping

When it comes to selling your franchise to prospective franchisees, your Franchise Proposition is essentially what you put in your "shop window". It will be the cornerstone of your franchise brochure, and as such it is your one chance to make a first impression.

It goes by various different names. For example, you may see it referred to as a "Franchise Package". Whether you put in a printed brochure, or an e-shot, or on an online franchise listing site, the proposition is your pitch to prospective franchisees. Drawing from the analysis you have done in your Franchise Development Plan, the proposition summarises what you are offering your franchisees, and what they are required to pay you for it. In terms of creating a first impression, the quality of presentation is critical. But likewise so is truth and accuracy. We will look at this in more detail in Step 4.

Franchisors present their Franchise Proposition in a variety of different ways. There is no set format. But the key elements are always:

> ➢ Your Start-Up Pack, the things that you are providing to help the franchisee to get started
> ➢ The Initial Training that you will provide
> ➢ The fees that you will charge the franchisee, both up front and throughout the term of the franchise
> ➢ The Franchisee's likely minimum total investment in the franchise
> ➢ The ongoing support that you will provide.

The Start-Up Pack

This is also sometimes referred to as a "Franchise Set-Up Package". As the names suggest, it is the bundle of things that you are providing to your franchisees in order to get them started. As we discussed earlier, a franchise should comprise a "business in a box". In other words, it is a turnkey package, giving a franchisee everything they need to set up and run a business according to an existing methodology or system. The more comprehensive the Start-Up Pack, the more consistency you will have across your franchised network. It may contain some or all of the following:

➢ Essential equipment - eg tools needed for each job
➢ IT equipment
➢ For retail concepts – fixtures and fittings
➢ Initial stock of products / merchandise
➢ Vehicle (or branded livery for the franchisee's own vehicle)
➢ Branded signage
➢ Marketing materials
➢ Initial stock of uniforms

It is increasingly common for some of these items to be provided online, particularly standard templates for marketing materials. The IT equipment may come in the form of a software licence.

If there are core items that the franchisee needs to acquire independently, and at their own cost, this will have to be made clear to them. We will in more detail at how to present the details of your franchise in Step 4.

Initial Training

Again, we will look at this in more detail in Step 4. But when preparing your Franchise Proposition, you will want to set out at least

- ➤ how long the training course takes
- ➤ what format it follows
- ➤ where it takes place
- ➤ what skills and knowledge with the franchisees gain from it.

What should you charge your franchisees?

Initial Fees and Ongoing Fees

There is no magic formula for setting fees. But some of the key things that you will want to consider are:

The need to create a profitable business

Having taken care to complete your Financial Analysis with accurate and realistic information, you have to set your fee structure so that both you and your franchisees are able to trade profitably. There are very few franchised concepts which are genuinely capable of generating profits from month one. Many concepts will not generate any profit or salary for the franchisee in their first 6 to 12 months. But bear in mind that the longer it takes your franchisees to earn decent returns from the business, the smaller your pool of prospective candidates, and the more difficult it will be to recruit them.

The challenge is harder for retail concepts, and other businesses (for example, such as gyms) where commercial premises are required. For premises based franchises, the set-up costs, including fit-out, property costs etc can be considerable. There is also a lead-time between incurring the cost of premises, and starting to trade. This can pose some particular cashflow challenges for franchisees, so it is essential that they have sufficient working capital.

A surprisingly common pitfall amongst new franchisors is that they underestimate the cost of recruiting and supporting their franchisees in the early stages, and therefore undercharge for it. Largely due to a lack of good forecasting, it is all too easy to set the fee levels too low, with the result that whilst the franchisee can – all things being well - make a return on their business, the franchisor does not.

Unless you are a charitable organisation, you should not launch a franchise unless you are confident that you will make money from it. You won't achieve that from day one, but you should be confident that you can do so in the long term, and that you have sufficient working capital to fund your existence in the meantime.

Franchisors who underestimate their own costs live to regret it. In an attempt to mitigate their losses, they have a tendency to cut back on the level of support they are providing. This in turn means that they do not deliver what they promised to their franchisees, leading to franchisee disappointment and sometimes even mutiny. Eventually the whole franchise can implode.

Compare yourself to your competition

You may want to buy-in some objectivity here, from an independent expert or adviser. As a new franchisor, you will naturally be enthusiastic and confident about the value that your franchise represents. But an independent advisor – whether a franchise consultant, your bank, your accountant or your lawyer – may well have more objectivity than you do as to how your proposition matches up to other competitor offerings.

Your specific industry sector is less relevant in this context. What is more important is what other franchise offerings are available at a similar start-up cost. This is the analysis that prospective franchisees will be making as they shop around, before deciding which concept to choose. Information on fees and set-up costs charged by other franchise systems is widely available online, on franchise listing sites and/or on the franchisors' own websites. This makes it relatively easy for you to see what other systems are offering, but at the same time your franchisees have plenty of opportunity to compare your offering against others.

Initial Fees

As the name suggests, these are charged by the franchisor for the start-up of the franchise. The Initial Fee is in most cases payable by the franchisee in full when they sign their agreement. Some franchises offer to take the Initial Fee in instalments, but this has obvious risks for the franchisor, so it is not a good choice for everyone. If the franchisee has already provided a deposit, then this would be set off against the Initial Fee, so that the franchisee pays the balance on signing their franchise agreement.

For the majority of franchised systems, the Initial Fee is set somewhere between £5,000 and £20,000. But some are less, and some are substantially more. Although there is no hard and fast rule as to setting Initial Fees, it is worth bearing in mind the approach taken by the British Franchise Association, which is that the Initial Fee should cover the cost of recruiting the franchisee, as well as the cost of their training and the cost of their start-up package. It is not intended to be a cash windfall. If it ends up lining the franchisor's pocket substantially, then in all probability the franchisor is cutting corners on training and support, and not providing the franchisee with good value for money.

Management Service Fees

These are the ongoing fees that the franchisee will pay you throughout the life of the franchise agreement. These are sometimes referred to as *"MSF"*, sometimes *"royalties"*, and sometimes *"franchise fees"*. We will refer to them here as Management Service Fees (or MSF for short).

Again, there are no specific rules as to how to set the MSF. Most typically, it is set as a percentage of the franchisee's total turnover (ex VAT). Anything between 5% and 10% is fairly common. The benefit of a percentage of sales is that it technically shares the risk and reward between franchisor and franchisee. In other words, the better the franchisee does in their business, the more money the franchisor receives in ongoing fees, and vice-versa. The ongoing fees are, so far as the franchisee is concerned, scalable according to the rate of growth of their business.

Some businesses, however, take an alternative view, and have a set monthly fee, so that the amount payable by the franchisee is fixed, regardless of how well (or otherwise) the franchisee is doing. The theory is that it gives franchisees more of an incentive, as the higher their turnover, the lower the MSF is in terms of a percentage of sales. Whereas a percentage MSF, on the other hand, is sometimes perceived as a *"penalty for success"*. As a general rule, however, a percentage-based MSF is going to be easier to sell to prospective franchisees, because the affordability (or otherwise) of it is likely to be more obvious. With a set MSF figure, a prospective franchisee will need some reassurance that his or her turnover figures are going to be sufficient. And if you are looking at bfa membership, the bfa will question you on a set MSF, as they will want to ascertain that it will be affordable for your franchisees.

Advertising Contributions

Some franchised businesses have an additional ongoing fee, in the form of a contribution towards a centralised marketing fund (sometimes called an *"Ad Fund"*, and sometimes a *"National Advertising Contribution"*), run by the franchisor solely for the purpose of marketing the brand. The franchisor will undertake not to spend these marketing contributions on anything other than marketing and promotion, and will provide franchisees an annual audited statement to that effect. But the franchisor will be free to spend it on whatever initiatives they think fit.

An Ad Fund contribution would typically be something in the region of 2% of franchisees' turnover. Again, there is no hard and fast rule. If you have an Ad Fund, you will calculate in your projections what impact this has on the franchisees' profitability, when added to the MSF that they are also paying.

Cost of supplies

There are a certain number of franchised systems which involve the franchisee acquiring all, or at least some elements of, their goods, equipment, services or raw materials from the franchisor. The franchisor thus has an additional revenue stream, in the form of the margin they make on the supply.

Although this sounds good from the franchisor's perspective, there are some pitfalls.

First and foremost, attempting to conceal from your franchisees the existence of a mark-up is dangerous. It causes significant feelings of bad faith when eventually the truth comes to light, and inevitably it will eventually.

Secondly, your supply of products, equipment or services needs to represent good value to the franchisee, both in the short and long term. It is reasonable for you to keep a margin for yourself, provided that your franchisees still get the products at or below the best price that they could source them anywhere else. Realistically, you will not be able to hold on to your franchisees, or force them to buy their supplies from you, if they can get better value elsewhere. This is regardless of whatever you purport to provide in your franchise agreement.

Thirdly, there are some anti-competition rules in the UK and Europe that put limitations on your right to specify a particular source of supply.

Franchisee Minimum Investment

A prospective franchisee will need to understand how much the franchise is going to cost them, not just in terms of Initial Fees but also their own start-up costs, and the amount of working capital required, over what period.

The "Minimum Total Investment" is, as the title suggests, the total amount of money that the franchisee will need to put into the business. The "Minimum Personal Investment" is the amount that the franchisee will need to have in their own unencumbered funds. Banks will limit the amount of funding that they provide. It is common for them to expect franchisees to personally fund at least 30% to 50% of the start-up costs from their own resources. If you have the support of a bank willing to provide funding for your franchisees, you will already know the percentage of the total cost that will be the franchisees' Minimum Personal Investment.

Ongoing support from the Franchisor

The proposition should address not just the initial start-up of each franchise, but also how the franchisor will continue to support the franchisee throughout the term of their franchise agreement. It is universally true that holding on to franchisees for the long term is nigh-on impossible unless they perceive that they continue to get value from their franchisor year in and year out.

One of the most commonly cited reasons for franchisee exits is that they feel that support from the franchisor effectively stopped after the set-up phase. The story is all too common: A franchisee benefits from the set-up, training and initial support that you have provided, and then sooner or later, with ideas of saving his or herself the cost of ongoing franchise fees, they abandon the franchise and set up a competing business of their own.

Your franchise agreement should bind your franchisees to the franchise for the duration of your franchise term, and it should also provide that a franchisee cannot, for a period of time after termination, compete with your franchised system, or continue to supply products or services to their franchise customer base. That is all good in theory. But practical reality is something else. Enforcement of non-compete clauses is notoriously difficult, and expensive. Having a comprehensive and competitive supply chain is one way of reducing the risk.

STEP FOUR – IMPLEMENTATION

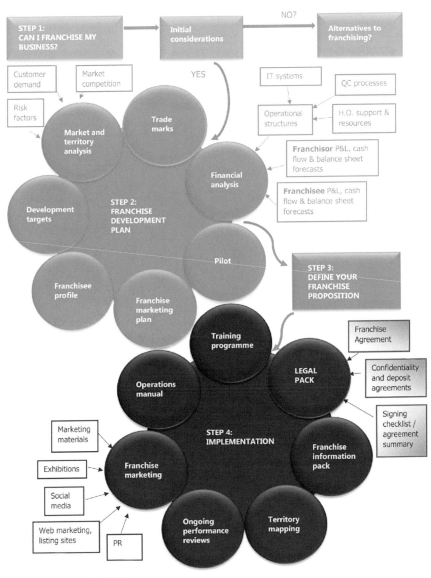

The Legal Pack

What does the legal pack contain?

Your legal advisers will provide you with a set of templates for the core legal documents that you need to support and protect your franchised business. The set should include a confidentiality agreement, a deposit agreement and a franchise agreement. Your advisers may also provide you with other supporting documents, such as a summary document, providing an overview of the key provisions of your franchise agreement. They may also provide you with a checklist for getting your agreements signed.

Whilst the confidentiality and deposit agreements tend to follow a standard form, the franchise agreement needs to be a bespoke document. Just as no two businesses are the same, likewise no two franchise agreements should be the same either. The form of the franchise agreement is explained in more detail below.

A professional and good quality franchise agreement, which protects your brand and your specific business needs, has to be genuinely tailor-made. It should be robust, properly protecting your legal position, whilst at the same time keeping a focus on the key issues that matter the most to your franchise system. You should therefore anticipate that it will cost a few thousand pounds.

The good news is that the fee should be more or less a one-off cost. You will present your franchise agreement to new franchisees as being "non-negotiable". The vast majority of franchisors will not enter into individual negotiations with franchisees over the form of the franchise agreement, and they will make that quite clear to potential franchisees during the course of the recruitment process. There are a couple of good reasons for this. Firstly, having spent a good sum of money on the agreement, you will not want to incur an ongoing cost paying your lawyers to pick their way through suggested amendments made by the lawyers acting for the franchisees. Secondly, though, you also want to ensure, as far as possible, that you are contracting with all your franchisees on the same terms.

You should therefore be able to cover the cost of the franchise agreement from your first few initial franchise fees, if you budget accordingly.

Who should draft your legal documents?

The importance of getting your franchise agreement right can scarcely be over-stated. Your franchise agreement underpins and protects your entire franchise concept. Even the most successful franchised systems will eventually have a legal dispute with one or more of their franchisees. So what your franchise agreement says really does matter, and it follows, therefore, that it matters who puts it together for you.

Do not believe anyone who offers you a blank template and tells you that it will be fine. You should also use a lawyer who is a franchise law specialist. The British Franchise Association's website lists a large number of affiliated franchise lawyers and law firms. We discuss bfa membership in more detail towards the end of Step 4, but even if you are not planning to join the bfa in the future, their list of franchised lawyers are the ones to look to.

Confidentiality agreement

The confidentiality agreement (often referred to as a Non-Disclosure Agreement, or NDA) is likely to be the first legal document that you give a prospective franchisee. Having reviewed your publicly available information, including your prospectus and/or franchise information pack, the prospect should sign a confidentiality agreement before you proceed to give them any further information.

Deposit agreement

The deposit agreement is sometimes combined with a deposit agreement. But it can be best to separate them. Depending on the recruitment process that you establish for your franchise, the deposit agreement can sometimes to come into play at a later stage. The deposit agreement is given to a franchisee at the point that you are asking them to pay a deposit towards their initial fee. This would typically be when the prospective franchisee is completing his/her final due diligence on you and your franchise opportunity.

The bfa expects that a deposit should be refundable if the franchisee decides not to go ahead, save that you can legitimately deduct your actual out-of-pocket expenses incurred in connection with that franchisee's recruitment process.

The franchise agreement

Your franchise agreement is provided to the franchisee once

they have made their decision to proceed, but before they do their initial training. The franchise agreement is detailed, and relatively long, because it contains all the franchisee's obligations to run the business in the manner that you specify. Typically, a franchise agreement will be at least 20,000 words, or 40 pages or so, in length. In some cases, they can be substantially longer than that.

A skeleton outline of a typical franchise agreement is at Appendix B at the back of this book. It gives you a broad idea of layout and content of a franchise agreement, but it is not suitable to be used. In due course you will need your lawyer to prepare an agreement which properly fits your business.

Note also that the bfa have a number of requirements as regards the content of your agreement. If you are considering bfa membership, you will need to ensure that you choose a legal adviser who has the right experience, and who is fully aware of the bfa's policies on a number of issues.

Although each franchise agreement is different, it will typically cover the following:

➢ A description of the rights being granted, whether or not there is an exclusive territory.
➢ The term of the agreement and renewal rights. Note that once your franchisee has signed up for, say, a 5 year initial term, he or she will have no right to terminate before the end of that initial term. To do so would leave them liable to you for your loss of fees (or profits) for the whole of the remainder of the term.
➢ The fees payable by the franchisee to you – how much, when and by what means

- Your initial obligations as regards setting-up the franchisee
- The training that you will provide, and what levels of training must be successfully completed before the franchisee can start their business.
- Your ongoing obligations, to support and assist the franchisee throughout the term of the agreement.
- The franchisee's ongoing obligations – note that this section will most likely take up the bulk of the content of your franchise agreement, and is the part which is the most "bespoke" for you. It will cross-refer to your operations manual, and these two documents will together set out a complete blueprint as to how the franchisee must run the business on a day to day level.
- The minimum performance criteria that the franchisee must achieve. This separate to any notion of ideal performance target that you may encourage your franchisees to achieve. The minimum performance criteria are (as the name suggests) the very lowest level of performance, below which you might well want to ask your franchisee to leave the system.
- Ownership of telephone numbers, domain names and social media accounts etc.
- Any requirement for the franchisee to have a business plan, and how this would be discussed and/or approved by you.
- Responsibility for advertising and promotion. What local marketing must the franchisee undertake? If you are going to collect and hold advertising contributions from franchisees for the benefit of your system as a whole, you will need to set out how you will apply them.

- The accounting records that the franchisee must keep and submit to you.
- Your rights in relation to your trade mark and the franchisee's permission to use it.
- The franchisee's right to sell the business, and your right to approve any buyer.
- The franchisee's obligations not to compete with you, or "steal" customers, either during or at the end of the franchise term.
- What happens on death or incapacity of the franchisee? Your right to manage the franchised business on their behalf if necessary.
- Your right to terminate if the franchisee is in breach, and what happens in relation to handing back the business on termination.
- Disclaimers of the franchisor's liability to the franchisee.
- A personal guarantee by the franchisee, if they are trading through a limited company.

Process for getting legal documents signed

Your legal advisers may offer to issue your franchise agreements on your behalf to franchisees. It is all too easy to make mistakes in this respect, and therefore it may well be worth taking up their offer in this respect.

It also makes sense to stress the need for franchisees to have their franchise agreement reviewed by an independent lawyer who is affiliated to the bfa. This will ensure that your franchisee understands what their legal obligations are, and also that these obligations are of a type which is typical in franchising.

Always make sure that your franchisee signs and returns the franchise agreement to you before they start operating the business. It is also important to ensure that you have safely stored a copy of the signed agreement, for future reference.

Operations Manual

Why do you need one?

The importance of your operations manual cannot be over-stated. It is the bedrock of your franchise system, and enshrines the unique elements and operating methods of your business that create your know-how.

Franchising is, of course, all about brand consistency. You expect that customers to be attracted to your brand, because they recognise it and trust it. They will trust it because they know that the products and services will be provided to a consistent standard, no matter which franchisee they are dealing with. The powerful presence, for example, of franchised coffee chains on British high streets is testament to this. Their customers are not particularly interested in whether they are dealing with a franchisee or not. It is the brand that they are associating with, their knowledge of the product offering and their expectations of good customer service.

It follows therefore that your franchisees need to deliver your franchise concept to their customers with meticulous compliance with a common set of instructions.

Taking the fast-food sector, by way of example: Not only does your menu range have to be the same in every outlet, but you also need to have detailed instructions as to how each menu item is prepared and served. It is no surprise that the operations manuals used by quick service restaurant concepts are hugely voluminous. Each type of burger has precise details of construction. Even down to things like the required weight of lettuce, and the positioning of each piece of pickle.

Together with your franchise agreement, your manual sets

out exactly how your franchisees are required to operate. Your franchise agreement has to give you the right to terminate your franchisee's operation if he or she is not acting in accordance with the operating manual. So the content of it is going to be crucial.

In times gone by, an operations manual was always a printed document, usually kept in a folder, requiring franchisees to add or substitute pages from time to time in line with updates made by the franchisor. More commonly now, the operations manual is maintained on a database or cloud system controlled by the franchisor. It usually contains a suite of separate documents, and sometimes refers the franchisee to specific government regulations that apply to the franchisor's particular industry.

Should you write it yourself, or can someone else do it for you?

The task of creating your operations manual can be a daunting one, particularly as there is no standard "template" that you can simply follow. The job is laborious, and new franchisors often, quite understandably, simply do not know where to start.

Franchise consultants and advisers who have experience in putting manuals together, can be of considerable help in this context. However, in practical terms you are unlikely to be able to outsource the job entirely. There will almost certainly be a large amount of collaboration between you and your advisers. Their skill and experience enables them to edit and finesse the content, and put it in a user-friendly format. They can also prompt you to cover elements that you may otherwise have overlooked. But as they do not live and breathe your business like you do, they will be reliant on you for a large amount of information and/or content.

Whether or not you engage a consultant to help you, do not underestimate the amount of your time and resources that will need to go into the creation of your operations manual. So it is wise to have considered this when you put your Franchise Development Plan together, at Step 2.

What should it contain?

There is no obligatory format for an operations manual. But ease of use is important. You will want it to be relatively straight-forward for franchisees to navigate their way around it.

New franchisors are sometimes disappointed to find that there is no such thing as an operations manual "template". Your business format is unique to you, and your process for supporting and interacting with your franchisees is not going to be the same as any other franchisor. Your operations manual really does need to be written specifically for you.

Some franchised systems have operations manuals which run to hundreds or even thousands of pages. Others manage with a much shorter document. But either way, it has to contain all the information that your franchisees need for the purposes of operating their business consistently in accordance with your methods.

Appendix A towards the back of this book has a sample of a contents page, to give you a general flavour of what your manual will need to contain. Bear in mind that it is by no means comprehensive. It provides you with a checklist of some of the key issues that tend to be covered in the manual. Your own manual will no doubt have some additional specific elements.

The content of your manual will in a number of ways reflect

your franchise agreement. The franchise agreement will cross-refer to the manual extensively. It makes sense to be working on your operations manual at the same time that work gets underway on your franchise agreement, and bear in mind that you will most likely adjust each of those documents, in light of what you decide to put in the other.

The good thing about the operations manual is that it has flexibility. Your franchise agreement is more or less set in stone at the moment that your franchisee signs it. But the operations manual can evolve over time. So long as your business remains fundamentally the same, you can change or add to your processes from time to time by publishing updates to your manual. This is easier from a logistical perspective if your manual is cloud-based. But either way, any changes must be communicated to your franchisees, and you will need to keep a record of those communications, in case any disputes arise later.

Training Programme

Why is this important?

It is easy to underestimate the significance of your franchisee training programme. Along with your brand and your support structure, your training is one of the key things that your franchisees are buying from you. It therefore needs to have perceptible value. Otherwise your franchisees will quickly become disillusioned with you and your system. Both your initial training programme, and your ongoing training, need to live up to the expectations that you set for the franchisee during their recruitment process.

One complaint frequently made by franchisees, in the course of a legal dispute with their franchisor, is that their training was not adequate. Often the complaint is that the initial training programme did not actually tell the franchisee anything that he or she could not have worked out for themselves. In other cases, the complaint is that after signing the franchise agreement and paying their Initial Fee, the initial training was sketchy, and the franchisee had to use their own initiative to source the know-how and skills that they needed.

It is through the training programme that you impart your vital know-how for the franchise. In terms of franchising being a "Business in a Box" (a concept which we looked at earlier in this book), the training tells the franchisee everything they need to know in order to run a successful business, exactly in accordance with your business format.

No matter how good your training programme is, you will inevitably need to devote a considerable amount of time on an ongoing basis to supporting and helping your franchisees. But the more comprehensive your training programme is, the easier it will be for you to manage and support your franchisees in the long term, and the more successful they will be.

Initial training and ongoing training

Your franchisees will do their initial training with you once they have signed their franchise agreement and paid their initial fee. If your franchisee does not do well in the initial training, and despite giving them some additional support, they genuinely cannot meet your required standards, your franchise agreement should provide that you have the right to terminate that franchisee's agreement. Typically, you would then refund the initial fee paid by the franchisee, less your actual out-of-pocket costs.

New franchisors sometimes get their initial training right, but then overlook the need for ongoing training, throughout the duration of each franchise. But your ongoing training is important for a few reasons:

- ➢ If a franchisee starts to under-perform, you need a mechanism for getting them back on course
- ➢ Ongoing training enables you to implement changes and updates to your operating methods from time to time
- ➢ The franchises that are the most successful are those which have ongoing innovation. If you impart the sum total of your know-how to your franchisees on day one of their franchise, and thereafter sit back, your franchisees will tend to conclude that they can run their business without you. Modifying and improving your system from time to

time to keep up with market changes or new technologies, and providing ongoing training, is one very good way of keeping your franchisees engaged.

What should your training programme contain?

This will depend entirely on the structure of your business and your industry sector. There are some commonly-recurring themes, and some of these are set out below. But otherwise there is no such thing as a "standard" franchise training programme. No matter what kind of business you are franchising, it will take some considerable time and resources to put your training materials together. In addition to the factual content, you will also want to think about how to make the learning manageable and engaging, and using which types of media for which elements. This can include a combination of:

> Talks
> Reading
> Round-table discussions
> Video
> E-learning
> Practical role-playing

Some of the training may be delivered in a class-room setting. You may want certain elements, however, to be out in the field – with the new franchisee shadowing you or an experienced franchisee whilst they are providing their goods/services to their customers.

Some franchise systems can comfortably fit all of their initial training into one or two weeks. But others can take significantly longer. Your franchisee will not be running their business during this time, or earning money. So the length of the training programme needs to be factored into the figures that you will be working on in your financial analysis in Step 2.

Your training programme will need to cover, amongst other things, the key elements of your operations manual. So you will most likely want to have your operations manual prepared first, before you start on your training programme.

Note that your training will also link closely to your franchisee recruitment criteria, which we looked at in Step 2. It makes sense to start with these criteria, and work forward from that to identify the key elements of learning that the franchisee will need to add, in addition to their existing skills and experience.

Importantly, your initial training needs to incorporate some form of assessment(s), so that you can officially pass or fail the franchisee at the end of the course, and if the franchisee doesn't pass, there needs to be a system for re-sitting the relevant elements.

Here are some of the key areas that you will almost certainly want to cover in your initial training:

> Process for setting up their business – bank accounts, standing orders, accountancy support
> Equipment/stock required
> Sources of supply
> Detailed description of the goods/services that the franchisee is providing to customers specifications and scope of services; product ranges; components
> Use of software and customer database
> Recommended pricing
> Customer terms & conditions
> Engagement of staff and contractors, terms & conditions
> Legal requirements eg health & safety; industry regulations; hygiene
> Processing orders and/or delivery of goods and services
> Accounting procedures, what financial information to record, and how to submit it to you
> How and when franchisees must make payments to you
> Quality standards and customer service; handling of customer complaints
> What to do, and who to contact, if problems arise

In addition to the above, many franchisors will want their franchisees to have a good understanding of the financial aspects of running a business. New franchisees often have little or no prior experience of running any kind of business on their own. In this respect, they have a steep learning curve ahead of them when they sign their franchise agreement. There is good sense in making sure that your franchisees are as financially literate as possible. You may well want to bring in external help to provide this element of training. No matter what industry sector they are in, franchisees should understand the basics of profit & loss accounts, balance sheets and cash flow forecasts. They should also be able to prepare and take ownership for their own business plans. The more responsibility they can take for this, the better.

Another critical area is sales and marketing. Almost any franchise concept will require its franchisees to find customers and sell to them. If the franchisee lacks basic selling skills, they will struggle to make a success of their business. Your initial training should tell your franchisees what profile of customer to look for, which marketing channels can enable the franchisee to reach them, and it should include appropriate selling techniques.

You will also want to ensure that your franchisees understand what marketing activity (if any) you carry out on their behalf, and what marketing they must do for themselves. If they are responsible for their own local marketing, they will need to know what local marketing activity has been shown to work best for your particular concept.

Your franchisees will have varying levels of understanding and experience of social media. Your initial training will need to cover this, and it is sensible for you to establish a clear social media policy for them to follow.

Your ongoing training programmes for franchisees are going to depend on your business sector and your system format. Largely, they should build on topics covered in your initial training, with deeper focus on key areas, and updating and refining your courses as your business develops and as your industry sector evolves.

One final thought on the subject of training: As it enshrines your know-how, it needs to be protected. We touched on the subject of copyright in Step 2. Whilst a detailed analysis of intellectual property rights is outside the scope of this book, it is almost certainly the case that there is copyright in your training materials. You need to be the owner of that copyright, and you need to have the appropriate copyright notices on your materials, so that your ownership is clear. Being a key element of your know-how, it may have substantial value, and you need to make sure that it is not infringed or misused by third parties.

Franchise Marketing and Recruitment

Having invested time, energy and cost in designing your business concept and planning a proposition for your franchisees, you will get to what may well be the biggest challenge of all – recruiting your franchisees.

Franchising is a competitive business. Broadly speaking, there are more franchise opportunities to be bought, than there are suitable franchisees to buy them. Unless you are exceptionally fortunate, suitable franchisees for your concept will not land in your lap without effort on your part. You will need to put resources into finding them and convincing them that your concept is right for them.

In your franchise recruitment efforts, you will be competing against a number of other franchise offerings. Bear in mind that a large proportion of franchises do not require prior experience in their particular industry sector, the whole point being that the franchise owner will train their franchisees in how to run the business. When it comes to franchise recruitment, therefore, your "competitors" are not just those businesses operating in your sector. Your competitors potentially include all the other concepts, in all sorts of sectors, and in particular those for which the franchise entry cost is similar to yours. And even beyond that, your potential franchisees might be looking at all sorts of opportunities, not necessarily only franchised ones. So when it comes to franchise recruitment, your pool of competitors is a lot wider than you might think.

You will also want to hold fast to your franchisee profile, which you will have looked at in Step 3. Tempting though it is, you cannot afford to compromise on the key criteria that you want your franchisees to meet. For all these reasons, you will be prepared to work hard at your franchise marketing, and budget accordingly.

There are a number of different channels for franchise recruitment. What works best for you is going to depend on a number of factors, including your ideal franchisee profile, their investment potential, and your business sector. There are some types of franchise – "mother and baby" groups being one of a number of good examples – where your pool of potential franchisees comes from your own customer base. If this applies to your business, you have an advantage. But even then, you will want to plan a suitable budget to reach out to a broader pool of candidates when you need to.

We look at some specific marketing channels below. Most well-established franchisors will take a multi-channel approach to franchise recruitment, rather than relying on one source of leads. Whatever channels you decide to use, you will need to ensure that your message and your branding are consistent throughout.

If you do not have branding, PR and marketing experience yourself, you will without question need to engage professionals to help you. A visit to any of the national franchise shows will demonstrate to you just how much resource and money franchisors invest in the presentation of their brands. In such a competitive landscape, your marketing is going to have to look at least as professional, smart and engaging as that produced by your competitors.

Sadly, under-investment in franchise marketing is one of the most common issues that cause new franchise concepts to fail. By the time you come to your marketing spend, you will already have invested substantial time and money in your franchise concept. You do not want to fall at the final hurdle, by not budgeting realistically for your marketing.

Franchise Marketing Materials

Franchise Information Pack

The franchise information pack is sometimes referred to as a franchise prospectus, or franchise brochure. It sets out key information about the business you run, and the franchise opportunity. The format of it varies from one franchise to another. It is often a glossy A4 leaflet, running to 10 to 20 pages or so, with a strong use of imagery and graphics. Its primary purpose is to present your brand, and your business ethos, in an appealing way to potential franchisees. Hence the need for your document to look slick and professional.

It will tend to have some broad information about the nature of the franchise proposition. There is no standard template for the prospectus. However, some of the things that you may include in the information pack are:

- ➢ What your business does
- ➢ Why it is successful
- ➢ Your values
- ➢ Why someone would want to invest in your franchise
- ➢ What the franchisee gets from you, in exchange for their fees
- ➢ Broadly, what it will cost the franchisee, in terms of initial fee, working capital, and ongoing fees. (Although some franchisors save this information for later on in the recruitment process.)

As the franchise information pack is a "public domain" document

– ie something that is not confidential – you would not expect to see detailed financial information in it. In particular, it would be highly unwise to include anything that amounts to a profit forecast. That is something that you may come to later on in your recruitment process, and then only in a manner which is very carefully controlled. It is also important that, whilst you want to make your franchise opportunity appear as appealing as possible, you avoid any form of over-selling. Your proposition, if thoroughly researched and prepared, should sell itself, without the need for exaggeration or embellishment.

An example franchise brochure is set out here, by kind permission of Right At Home. (All rights reserved.)

www.rightathomefranchising.co.uk

WELCOME TO RIGHT AT HOME - THE CARE FRANCHISE
BUILT AROUND QUALITY

This brochure will address the 7 fundamental questions you need answering when evaluating the life changing decision to start a new business and to make a difference every day

Question 1: What exactly does Right at Home do?

Provides a premium quality service to adults and older people who require some assistance to live at home and enjoy their independence

Operates predominantly in the private sector, following a business model quite different to that delivered by Government sponsored care

Delivers highly-personalised support that benefits the whole family, not just the individual Client. Your care team would offer companionship, social activity, support with diet, exercise and household management, as well as personal care and help with mobility

Keeps the Client's well-being as the top priority. The Right at Home approach of using consistent and thoughtfully-matched carers, who ideally visit for at least one hour, promotes strong relationships, trust and a holistic approach to the Clients' care and quality of life

❝ It is such a welcome surprise to employ a care agency that does what they say they will provide, plus much more. My mother is now getting the support she should get, far better and streets apart from the variable care previously given by two other care agencies. My role is already starting to change back, where possible, to being my mother's daughter. ❞

- P. W. Daughter of Right at Home Client

In 2015 100% of Right at Home offices had a good or outstanding rating from The Care Quality Commission Regulatory Body (CQC)

Question 2: How does Right at Home work?

We give you what we believe is the **highest quality opening package** in the industry, containing all you need to get your business up and running

We give you **comprehensive initial training** that covers every aspects of the business. We support you in the recruitment of an experienced Registered Care Manager, so you don't need prior experience of care

We guide you through the start up and registration process so you can move into a new sector with confidence, knowing you are backed by the expertise of a highly experienced and respected franchisor

While your Registered Care Manager oversees operations, you will be responsible for strategic planning, establishing your business in the local community, networking, hosting events and building relationships with potential referral sources

With our support, you will implement marketing and recruitment strategies that reflect the quality of your services and promote your business as a great place to work, enabling you to meet **structured growth** targets

Once your reputation is established, your role will focus more on the **business development** and **controlled expansion** into your whole territory

> The training has been so valuable - I can't speak highly enough about it. It can all seem a bit overwhelming at the start, but I couldn't have asked for more help and not once did I think I was being a nuisance. Having no specific "sector experience", it was a relief to see the scope of the experience within the team as well
> - Andrew Davis, Owner, Right at Home Bournemouth

92% ☆☆☆☆☆

Of our franchisees would rate the initial training as "good", "very good" or "excellent"

Question 3: What makes Right at Home stand out?

Right at Home UK acheived Full Membership of the British Franchise Association (bfa) after just three years of franchising and Right at Home Uk Managing Director, Ken Deary now sits on the British Franchise Association board of Directors.

In 2014 we were proud to become the very first **bfa Emerging Franchisor of the Year**, with judges praising our "unerring ethos of care quality and extraordinary franchisee results.

bfa Director General, Brian Smart said : "Right at Home impressed with the level and quality of support to franchisees... they've built a road to success neither cutting costs nor compromising on quality."

Two years later we won of the most coveted accolades in the franchise sector, the 2016 Best Franchise Award, which is based on franchisee satisfaction as well as performance.

EXCEPTIONAL LEADERSHIP

Managing Director, Ken Deary is a hands-on franchisor who has not only "walked the walk" in his previous career as a franchisee but won the highest possible accolade for a UK franchise owner, the British Franchise Association Individual Franchisee of the Year Award, during his time with McDonalds

Ken's successful growth and management of multiple locations also won him the coveted Golden Arches Award, given to the most successful McDonalds owners around the world. He has run a successful residential care business since 2006. Ken is also a board member of the BFA.

This proven success in franchising and experience in the care sector is unique to the UK home care franchise market, and has given Ken a true understanding of what the franchise owners want from their franchisor

His passion, drive and commitment to his franchisees' success are evident and as well as supporting existing franchisees, Ken oversees the recruitment of new owers from the first meeting to the final decision

❝ I think most Right at Home franchisees would agree that Ken's experience, honesty, integrity and ambition were a key factor in deciding to join this company rather than one of their competitors ❞

- Tim Haigh, Owner, Right at Home Sutton and Epsom

Question 4: What makes Right at Home unique?

QUALITY Our focus is having the best franchisees providing the best services, not the most franchisees working the most territories

BRAND Right at Home is a global leader in the Home Care sector with 500+ offices operating across 4 continents and a reputation for exceeding expectations

PEOPLE We make certain are owners are well-suited to the business and share our values, and then we make their success our priority

GROWTH Our focus on finding quality franchisees mean you join a highly-engaged and mutually supportive network. And because we take a measured growth strategy that means you receive excellent support staff ratios

ETHICS Right at home offers long-term profitability by way of building a scalable business in a large territory area. With a renewable 10 year franchise term and plenty of room for expansion, there need be no ceiling to your success

SUPPORT With compliance, marketing, recruitment, finance and all aspects of the business. Right at Home will work with you, visiting your office, holding regular conversations and inviting you to join webinars, regional meetings, strategy days and a two-day annual conference where you can share best practice and explore innovations. Our approach is to mentor, encourage and inspire you and the nature of our support evolves along with the growth of your business

Question 5: What's my investment and my return?

Franchise Fee	£31,995 + VAT
Working Capital Requirement	Up to £80,000
Royalty Payments	6.25% of Turnover + VAT (7.5% inc)
Average Time to Break Even	Approx Month 12
Approximate Gross Profit	Circa 40%
Approximate EBITDA	8-15% before owner's draw, for an established owner
Territories	All contain at least 35,000 over 65's
Franchise Term	10 Years, then 5 years repeat renewal

FINANCIAL SUPPORT

You will receive a complete business planning service, covered by the franchise fee, and benefit from our great relationship with HSBC, Natwest and Lloyds

If you are seeking maximum 70% bank funding, you will need to invest approx £37,000 of your own capital

We work closely with prospective franchisees to help them secure the best possible finance package

100%
Of our franchisees agreed if they could turn back time, they would invest in a Right at Home franchise

Question 6: What does the future hold?

Right at Home has become a key player in the private care sector since launching in the UK in 2010. We aim to become the **first-choice quality care brand** as we continue to meet our growth targets

The demand for quality care provision in the home had never been higher and because our population is ageing at an unprecedented rate, demand will only increase

The market is moving away from the traditional model of short-duration, task-led visits, towards person-centered models which promote good health and can ease pressure on the NHS by preventing repeat hospitalisation and bed-blocking

Government-funded care now allows for people to manage and top-up their local authority budgets, making quality care companies accessible to many more people

Group turnover for Right at Home UK doubled from 2014 to 2015 and we anticipate a similar scale for the next few years

All these factors mean there has never been a better time to enter a quality home care market

Question 7: What happens next?

We hope that what you've just read leaves you feeling intrigued and excited about the potential to make a difference in your community with Right at Home

To explore this opportunity further, just pick up the phone, visit our website or send us an email and take the next steps to making a difference every day.

Our evaluation process includes:

Informal initial conversations - discuss territory options and gain further insight through phone calls with our Franchise Recruitment Co-ordinator, Kate Dilworth

Discovery Day - Come and meet the Head Office Team and receive detailed information about Operations, Business Tools and Performance, Training and Support and Raising Finance

Interviews - we get to know you via in-depth telephone interviews with the Senior Management Team

Meet existing franchisees - a process of independent validation in which you can visit or speak to up to five franchisees of your choice

Regular review and support calls - we will speak regularly while you complete your due diligence to share information and address any areas of concern

Qualification Day - your opportunity to present the outcomes of your due diligence in a Right at Home business proposal and show us that you have what it takes to become a successful franchisee

Approval - A 10% deposit of the Franchise Fee is taken with a signed Letter of Intent to secure your territory, and we begin our RightStart Programme as soon as you are ready to proceed

WE LOOK FORWARD TO HEARING FROM YOU

Kate Dilworth, Franchise Recruitment Co-ordinator

Telephone : 0151 305 0755
Email : franchising@rightathomeuk.com
Website : www.rightathomefranchising.co.uk

" Joining Right at Home has been a great decision as they share my commitment to the highest standards of care and ethics for their clients "
- Michelle Apostol, Owner, Right at Home Twickenham

Franchise Disclosure Document

The term Franchise Disclosure Document appears often, but this is most typically in the context of countries where there is a statutory requirement for franchisors to disclose specific types of information to prospective franchisees, and/or where there is a legal requirement for franchises to be registered with a governmental authority. The USA is one good example, although there are a number of other countries that have mandatory disclosure and registration requirements. In a US context, the term "Franchise Disclosure Document" (or FDD) typically refers to a rather weighty and lengthy document. It is often produced in a slightly dry and indigestible format.

It is important to note that the UK is not regulated in this way. There is therefore no statutory requirement for UK franchisors to produce a formalised Franchise Disclosure Document. There are UK franchisors who will choose to do so, for a variety of reasons. Whilst this is an option, it is not compulsory.

Other Disclosures

Once a franchisor has provided the prospective franchisee with a franchise information pack, and got past this initial information stage, the form and context in which further, more detailed information is provided will vary considerably from one franchisor to another. This should ideally form part of a structured franchisee recruitment process, which you will formalise over a period of time.

One key issue is ensuring that confidential information - including detailed financial information - is not given to your prospective franchisee until they have signed and returned the confidentiality agreement, referred to earlier in this chapter.

It can be difficult to sell a franchise opportunity to a prospective franchisee without giving them some forecast of the likely level of profit that they will make from the business. Every prospect will ask you about this, and a refusal to give them any indication at all will very often drive them away. Realistically, you will have to be ready to give them some broad idea.

However, extreme caution is required when it comes to giving financial forecasts. You may choose to prepare forecast P&Ls for your prospective franchisees, showing them what their turnover, overheads and profits are likely to be over, say, years 1 to 5 of their franchise. Alternatively, you may provide your franchisee with a template, enabling them to complete their own figures. Either way, you carry some risk of a claim for misrepresentation against you, which arises if the franchisee later finds that the expected profits do not materialise. Your risk here is particularly high where your prospective franchisees have little or no prior business experience. Some key tips for managing your risks with financial forecasts are as follows:

> Avoid using aspirational figures. Wherever possible, base your figures on actual, past performance.
> Make it clear where your figures come from. Eg, do they come from the results of a pilot operation, or are they the average figures achieved by your other franchisees in the last 12 months?
> Do not rely on a blanket disclaimers in a footnote to your forecasts. A disclaimer is never a "get out of jail free" card. As it may in reality provide you with little or no protection against a legal claim, a blanket disclaimer can give you a

false sense of security.

- ➢ Err on the side of caution. If performance in one part of the country is better than in another, base your projections on the lower figures. Allow a suitable margin for error, to account for things like fluctuations in the economy.
- ➢ Encourage your prospective franchisees to seek independent financial advice before they commit to the franchise.
- ➢ Make sure that your franchisees prepare their own business plan before they sign up.
- ➢ Encourage your prospective franchisees to speak to as many of your existing franchisees as they want, so that they can get a broad picture of your network as a whole.

How and where should you market your franchise?

This is a trickier question than it used to be. In times gone by, there were a limited number of routes to franchise marketing. The main routes to franchise recruitment were franchise exhibitions, trade press and franchise magazines. In each case, the franchisor had a high degree of control over what information was available to prospective franchisees, and the franchisees had limited opportunities for doing their own research.

The advent of online marketing and social media has fundamentally changed the way that franchisees choose their franchises. Franchisors need internal and/or external resources to manage their brand presence in an online world. They also have to accept that the flow of information to prospective franchisees is no longer entirely within their control. They will in all likelihood have to manage a number of different communication channels, without necessarily having any clear certainty as to which have been more influential or successful.

Print media still has its place in some contexts. Particularly if you are seeking franchisees who have a specific industry qualification or background, and there is trade press which is targeted at people with your particular franchisee profile. But generally speaking, when it comes to marketing franchise opportunities, print advertising has largely been overtaken by online advertising, in its various forms.

We look at various marketing channels below. Whichever routes you choose, you will need specialist advice on setting suitable budgets, and establishing a marketing calendar. The timing of your marketing efforts is critical. Not least because you need to have the resources to handle enquiries when they come in. To make the most of your franchise marketing, you will want to be responding to enquiries pretty much immediately. You will want to avoid interest arriving in clumps, and that therefore necessitates scheduling it carefully in advance.

Online Marketing

Organising a coherent online marketing strategy that includes your website, paid online advertising, organic searches, online franchise listing sites and social media is a daunting task. The bad news is that you are very unlikely to be in a position to manage it effectively on your own. The world of online marketing simply moves too fast, and changes too quickly, for anyone other than online marketing specialists to keep up with it. On the other hand, the good news is that there are a number of well-qualified professionals who can advise you, and who specialise particularly in franchise marketing.

You will need a realistic budget, not just for setting up your website and online marketing, but for continuous review and adaptation, across all online channels. Your website may look fresh and up to date today, but it will not do so in three years' time unless you keep spending money on it, and this ongoing cost needs to be built into your franchise development plan.

➢ Your website

When it comes to franchise marketing through your website, you have two potential ways of doing it. The first is that you add a "franchising" click-through on your site, which takes the viewer to a separate franchising page or pages. The second, which is currently more commonly recommended by franchise marketing professionals, is that you have an entirely separate site aimed specifically for franchise recruitment.

The first option can be easier and cheaper, but the risk is that you mix your messages. It is true that your brand image, and the presentation of your brand values, should be the same for both customers and franchisees. But the specific messages that you want to send to each may be different. Furthermore, flagging up on your consumer-facing site that you have franchises for sale, can confuse customers about the consistency of your products or services.

Either way, you will need to work with your website developers to get the right solution.

> Website marketing

Website marketing can come in the form of Search Engine Optimisation (SEO), where the aim is to get high page rankings on search engines through organic means, or Paid Advertising, such as Google Pay Per Click (PPC) campaigns.

The complexity and ever-evolving nature of online marketing is such that it is virtually impossible to manage it without expert external support. For franchisors looking to promote their franchise opportunities to prospective franchisees, however, there are a number of franchise listing sites, with varying amounts of traffic, and these can prove to be more useful and cost-effective in terms of driving leads than website marketing initiatives.

> Franchise listing sites

There are a number of different franchise listing sites. They differ from one another in terms of pricing structure, total traffic volumes, and the number of leads generated. So it pays to shop around and research carefully. There is no "one size fits all" when it comes to franchise listing sites. What works very well for one franchise may work less well for another, so there is inevitably a level of trial and error involved.

Nick Strong is a director of **Franchise Intelligence**, working with franchisors to increase their return on investment in franchise recruitment.

Nick has seen that the advent of social media and website marketing has led to a significant shift in buyer behaviour in recent years. He notes that some franchisors have struggled to keep up with the changing landscape for franchise recruitment.

"Before the advent of online marketing and social media," says Nick *"it was the seller - the franchisor, in this case - who called the shots in the buying (or franchise recruitment) process. The franchisor controlled what information was disclosed to prospective franchisees, when and how, and in what format. A prospective franchisee would read a franchise brochure, prepared by the franchisor. They may see the franchisor exhibiting at a franchise show. They may attend a Discovery Day. But in each case, the franchisee is being presented with information about the franchisor that has been designed by the franchisor itself. A prospective franchisee might take some advice from family, workmates, friends, or local advisors. But he or she would otherwise be making a life-changing commitment, and a significant financial investment, on the basis of little else other than the selected information the franchisor chose to impart."*

Nick has found that the last few years have seen a marked shift. *"Potential franchisees have a level of scepticism, particularly when considering one of the vast majority of franchised systems, where the franchise brand name and business concept are not already common-knowledge. Potential franchisees are less likely to invest in a franchise without having carried out their own independent "due diligence" on the opportunity. These potential franchisees will view information provided by the franchisor as just one of a number of sources of knowledge. A franchisee will therefore look at all manner of sources of information that are now available to them."*

Nick points to a number of examples of different sources of information about a franchise: These might include:

The franchisor's website

- ➢ Facebook, Twitter and other social media channels operated by the franchisor
- ➢ LinkedIn and social media channels operated by the directors/owners of the franchise personally
- ➢ What customers and/or franchisees are saying, good and bad, about the franchise on social media
- ➢ TrustPilot and other review sites
- ➢ "Googled" information and opinion relating to the franchisor, its staff, owners and customers
- ➢ Information freely available at Companies House.

"You can control some of these sources," says Nick *"but not all of them."*

Nick explains that it is quite common for a potential franchisee to have carried out a substantial amount of due diligence on one or more franchise opportunities, without the franchisors in question having any awareness of it.

Nick's view is that franchisors should focus on their online reputation at the earliest possible stage. Here are his top tips:

"1. Consider developing your online presence well before you come to be marketing your franchise opportunity. Franchisors need to be gathering an online following, through social media and other online sources, which substantiates and endorses your franchise marketing messages.

2. Ensure that the owners of your business know how to use social media comfortably. Outsourcing this job to external suppliers, or delegating the job to someone junior in your organisation, can do more harm than good. It can mean handing your corporate voice to someone who has the least experience of your business.

3. Accept that your marketing messages will have to be communicated over a number of different online media, including listing sites, website marketing and social media. Because of franchisees' typically fragmented research processes, it will not be obvious right away which channels work for your business, and which don't." Nick advises that you choose your channels and then use them consistently for at least 3 to 6 months, measuring your results carefully. *"You can add to or subtract from these channels gradually, but only once you have allowed time to measure and review."*

Exhibitions

Anyone thinking about setting up a franchise concept is wise to go and visit one or more of the major franchise exhibitions that take place across the UK each year. The British Franchise Association sponsor a number of them, so it is worth looking at **www.thebfa. org** to see what is coming up near you.

A walk around one of these shows will demonstrate just how much effort and resource franchisors put behind the presentation of their franchise opportunity. Franchise shows can be expensive, so before you commit to one, you need to be confident that your own offering can stand up well against the competition.

Furthermore, you need to pick the right show to go to. The profile of visitors will vary from one show to another, and the more research you do on this before you commit, the better. The organisers of each show ought to be able to give you important demographic information about attendees. Crucially, you want to see data not just on total numbers of visitors, but the number of prospective franchisees visiting who have the right level of capital to invest in your business. Some show organisers will have profiled that information year on year, and will be able to give you some very reliable data.

The show's organisers should also give you an idea about how many good franchisee leads you are likely to get from the show. Bear in mind, of course, that on its own this information can be misleading. Some of the people you meet at shows may already have researched you fairly thoroughly in advance, and they may visit your stand simply to confirm a view about you that they had already provisionally reached. Others may look at your stand, pick up your literature, and even hear you speak at a seminar at a show, without actually making contact with you. They may come back to you later, perhaps prompted by other communications from you, and you may never know how much they were influenced by having seen you at the show.

The fact remains that national franchise shows are expensive, and if you are going to pay to be at one, you really do have to be thoroughly organised, not just at the show itself, but also before and afterwards, in order to maximise the benefit of being there. You need PR in advance of the show to encourage people to come to see you. You need a well-organised follow-up process after each show, so that contacts do not get lost or ignored. And you need to make sure that your stand at the show is staffed by positive people with good interpersonal skills. Visitors will be alienated by hard-sell tactics. But equally, if the people on your stand look bored, tired, hung-over, or distracted with emails on their devices, you would frankly be better off not being there at all.

Bear in mind that, apart from franchise shows, there are other exhibitions that might work well for your industry sector. These might be particularly good where your franchisees need to have specific industry or technical qualifications – eg hairdressing, as just one example. There are also a variety of shows aimed at new business start-ups. But whichever type of show you might be considering, the key is getting good demographic information about attendees, before you commit to exhibiting.

Public Relations

The benefits of engaging specific PR support are often under-estimated. Good PR advisers will raise your profile, not just through social media but also through a variety of different platforms which are pertinent to your industry or to your required demographic.

As social media forms such a key component of any PR strategy, you either need to be skilled at getting eye-catching messages out to your target audience, or otherwise you need to buy the expertise of an external agency.

Franchise Recruitment Process

Having decided on your channels for franchise marketing, and established a suitable budget and a marketing calendar, your next task is to establish a robust process for handling enquiries and managing franchise recruitment. We looked at setting a franchisee profile and recruitment criteria in Step 2. But setting the criteria will not be enough in itself. Once enquiries come in, you will need a process which ensures that you (i) make the most of each franchisee enquiry, while (ii) focusing the biggest proportion of your time and energy on those enquiries that appear to have the best prospects.

There is no template solution to this, and franchisors have differing approaches. But all franchisors find that their processes evolve over a period of time. The common thread is that all franchisors will make mistakes, particularly in the early stages. The important thing is to learn from the mistakes and adapt your process accordingly.

The stages of your recruitment process can include any of the following:

- ➢ Provision of an initial information pack, either a hard copy by post, and/or a pdf downloadable via your website
- ➢ Emails or telephone calls to acknowledge initial enquiries
- ➢ Questionnaires to establish the individual's suitability against your recruitment criteria
- ➢ Discovery Days – where you organise to see groups of interested individuals together, giving them an outline of what you are offering

- ➢ Face to face meetings and interviews
- ➢ Reviewing a business plan produced by the prospective franchisee.

It is a challenge, of course, to keep "good" prospects interested, without annoying people by bombarding them with information that they are not so interested in. You will need to evolve your own system of sorting the "wheat from the chaff" at an early stage. You need to be mindful that each prospect might have made approaches to several franchise businesses at once. So if you delay in following up with them, you will lose them. But at the same time, looking too desperate to "sell" your franchise will put people off, and furthermore it will waste your time.

Expense Reduction Analysts (ERA) are a well-established franchisor, with a carefully defined recruitment process. Overleaf (reproduced by ERA's kind permission) is an example of how they explain their recruitment process to potential franchisees:

ERA Recruitment Process

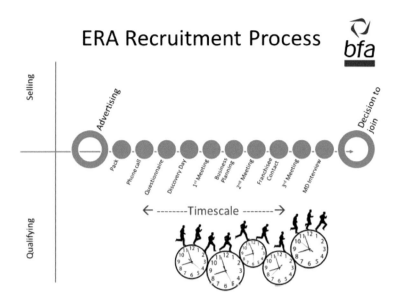

Territory Mapping

Why does territory mapping matter?

To maximise the commercial potential of your concept, you need to reach as many potential customers as you can. You want your franchisees to have a healthy amount of business, but you don't want them to have so much that they cannot service it effectively. There are franchise concepts that work better in one part of the country than in another. Even within the same county, there will be areas which are well-populated with suitable customers, and other areas that are less so.

If your franchisees will need to be visiting their customers locally, you are very unlikely to have a good picture of how many customers your franchisee can realistically reach in any one postcode, compared to another. Likewise, if you have a retail concept, the distance that customers are prepared to travel to reach you may vary substantially, even between two adjacent postcodes.

Public transport, size and location of shopping centres, positioning of schools, and even the positioning of main roads and motorways, can have a substantial impact.

If your franchise is based on exclusive territories (as most are) the size and demographic features of each territory can make the difference between a profitable franchise and a loss-making one. Even for those concepts that do not have exclusive territories, demographics still matter. Apart from anything else, without reliable data you will not know how many franchisees you should be aiming for.

Can you do your own territory mapping?

No matter how broad your business experience is, when it comes to territory mapping, you are very unlikely to have the expertise and knowledge. If you launch a territory-based franchise without getting some professional help with territory mapping, you will be launching your franchise on guesswork, and you will not ever know for sure if you have planned your franchise development in the most advantageous and profitable way.

Stuart Lee is Sales and Marketing Director for **Atlas Mapping**, one of the professional firms in territory mapping.

In terms of some of the common mistakes that franchisors can make, Stuart says:

"The single biggest regret I hear from developed franchisors is that the territories awarded in the early phases of franchising are substantially larger than is required. Be this either geographically too large for a franchisee to cover or that the territory contains too many potential customers for a franchisee to fully service the area. This results in lost earnings for the franchisor, and because the territory is protected within a franchise agreement, it is extremely difficult to regain any of this territory to set up another franchise.

Very often there is a mindset that being a developed franchisor with some territories that are too large would a "nice problem to have", I must say I am yet to hear a developed franchisor refer to it in that way!

The reality is that if the territories you award are not sufficiently planned or suitable for your business model, at some point in the future you will be forced to turn away great potential franchisees. These may go on to join your competitor's networks and capture the opportunity you are missing out on.

My advice on this subject would be to carry out some research on your existing trade areas to understand the composition of the market demographics. This data can then be brought together with your customer data to understand how well you are penetrating a market and what you can realistically expect a franchisee to cover."

Atlas Mapping help franchisors with consultancy to determine a realistic approach to territory mapping. The work involves carrying out a geographic analysis of existing trade areas and reviewing multiple examples throughout the country to check how the territory model will work.

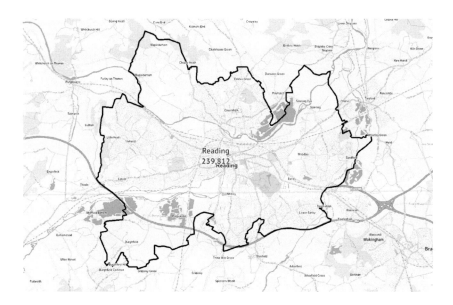

An example territory map

© Atlas Mapping 2016

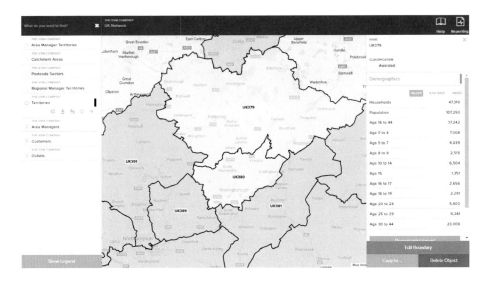

Screenshot of territory mapping software.

© Atlas Mapping 2016

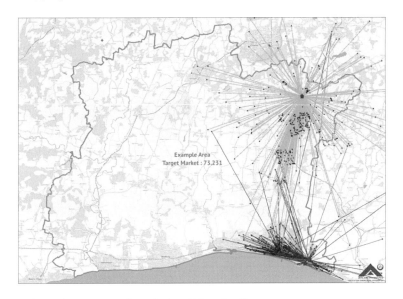

An example customer spread analysis within a territory

© Atlas Mapping 2016

"Working in this way," says Stuart "allows a mapping company to then pre-define an entire network of territories. Each territory will contain enough commercial opportunity for a franchisee to be successful and also demonstrate the correct number of territories available in an area. A professionally designed pre-defined territory network exposes the true number of territories in an area and helps franchisors avoid over committing to a single franchisee. It is important to note that a professional territory network will identify where you **cannot** take your franchise as there is not enough opportunity.

Additional to territory mapping services, there is web based software to help franchisors manage franchise territories and view detailed demographic market data. With simple access to this information, a franchisor and franchisee are able to come together with a shared understanding of the opportunity within a territory. Software has made access to key market data an integral part of the franchise recruitment process and improving the business planning of new franchisees.

ATLAS
MAPPING.

The right software and a professionally designed territory network provides a franchisor the structure to achieve the full potential of the brand."

Should you join the British Franchise Association?

About the British Franchise Association

The British Franchise Association **(bfa)**, formed in 1977, is a self-regulatory body for the UK franchise industry. Franchisors and professional advisers who meet the bfa's standards are allowed to become members. In addition, since 2012, it has been possible for franchisees who are part of a bfa member franchised system to become members as well.

The bfa is widely viewed as the voice of ethical franchising in the UK. In promoting ethical standards, its purpose is to act in the interests of the UK franchising industry as a whole, assessing and accrediting franchise companies which meet its criteria, and helping to ensure that the industry continues in the UK o develop credibility, influence and favourable circumstances for growth.

The bfa have a strict standards-based approach to membership. The bfa will only give accreditation to franchise concepts which can demonstrate that:

 - ➢ They have a *viable* product or service with a profit margin that will sustain a franchised network
 - ➢ The know-how of the business is *transferable* at arm's length to a franchisee
 - ➢ The business has *ethical* standards, complying with the European Code of Ethics for Franchising
 - ➢ All material information about the franchise proposition is clearly *disclosed* to prospective franchisees.

The bfa does not charge any application fee or joining fee, but members who are accepted must pay an annual subscription. The rates are published on the bfa's website **www.thebfa.org**.

If you are accepted for membership of the bfa, you will be expected to comply with the bfa's ethical standards. These are explained in detail in The Guide to the Code of Ethics, published by the bfa. You will also be required to follow (amongst other things) the bfa's Disciplinary Procedure and Complaints Procedure.

Do you have to be a member of the bfa?

Membership of the bfa is not obligatory. As the bfa is a self-regulating body for the UK franchise industry, franchisors and franchise professionals can choose whether or not to join. True enough, there are lots of franchised systems in the UK that are not bfa members. Some have simply chosen not to. Others have tried and failed to meet the bfa's criteria for membership.

Membership provides some substantial potential benefits. The bfa will require you to have at least some history of trading behind you before you can join, and the details of this are all set out on their website. Your application is therefore unlikely to go in until some time after you have launched your franchise. Nevertheless, it makes good sense to include it in your plans and your budget.

What are the benefits of bfa membership for franchisors?

Membership of the bfa is not obligatory, and there are lots of franchised systems in the UK that are not bfa members. But membership can be hugely beneficial in a number of respects, including the following:

- ➢ It adds to your credibility. Whilst bfa membership can never be an absolutely guarantee of excellence, it is clear that anyone who has achieved membership has at the very least met some fairly extensive criteria for membership.
- ➢ It indicates to your prospective franchisees that you intend to operate your system in an ethical and fair manner. In an increasingly competitive market, potential franchisees will be weighing up your franchise offering against various others. Bfa membership will be one of the factors that may add to the appeal of your concept over that of your competitors. Bearing in mind the challenge that franchisee recruitment can pose for franchisors, this can be a major plus point.
- ➢ Your franchise listing will appear on the bfa's website. With more than 20,000 unique hits per month, the bfa website directs over 200,000 visitors per year to its members' websites, so your membership gives your business visibility, and supports your franchise recruitment efforts.
- ➢ It provides regular networking events, opportunities for knowledge sharing and access to training programmes (including the bfa's Qualified Franchise Professional Programme (QFP)
- ➢ It provides PR opportunities, through speaking events and publication of your news stories on the bfa website and social media.

What are the benefits of bfa membership for franchisees?

Since 2012, the bfa has offered membership opportunities for franchisees. This can:

- ➤ Help your franchisees to gain financing, as specialist banks in the franchising sector will look positively on bfa accreditation
- ➤ Provide education, training and support opportunities for your franchisees.

Louise Harris is Franchise Director at **Wilkins Chimney Sweep**

Wilkins Chimney Sweep started franchising in 2011 having spent a year working with bfa accredited consultants and solicitors to finalise the model. Louise feels that it Wilkins benefits significantly from its bfa membership.

Louise says *"during our recruitment process we ask franchisees where they have seen us advertised and what was important to them in choosing a franchise. Without exception our franchisees have stated bfa as a deciding factor."*

She continued *"we're a small and quirky business. We know we can offer a bona fide system and great opportunity for franchisees, but having bfa accreditation simply ticks a box for our applicants and brings them over the threshold to the next stage.*

As a franchisor, membership is invaluable as it gives us access to best practice – ideas for supporting and helping the franchisees, legal guidance – and sometimes just peers who listen and can help guide choices.

Wherever possible we use bfa accredited suppliers. They understand the industry, how to work with us or the franchisees. It's just easier. As a new franchisor, they bring excellent ideas to us that we hadn't even considered and together make us better.

I found such value from the bfa membership that I put my name forward and was elected as an associate member representative on the board of the bfa. Now I have the chance to influence my industry as well."

FINAL CONSIDERATIONS

Funding Options for Franchises

If your franchisees will need bank funding to support their new business, it is well worth talking to one of the banks who have specialist teams focused on franchising.

Mark Scott is Director, Franchise Development in the **NatWest & RBS Franchise Team.** Mark has many years of experience advising and lending to franchised businesses.

"When franchisors approach us to discuss financing for them or their franchisees", says Mark Scott, of the NatWest & RBS Franchise Team, *"I am looking first and foremost, for honesty and integrity. I need to see how they have been trading to date, with real and comprehensive figures. I also like to see what challenges the franchisor has had in the past, and how they have overcome them.*

If the franchisor wants to borrow from the bank to set the franchise up, then we need to see that they can provide a good proportion of the capital that they need themselves. Because any new franchise start-up is inevitably speculative, at least to some extent, we would generally expect the franchisor to cover 50% of the funding. We also need to know that their core business will be able to repay the borrowing, even if the franchisor fails to recruit any franchisees." "Almost all our franchisee lending is in relation to systems where we have already developed a relationship with the franchisor, so we know their business, and the likely turnover, overheads and net profit of their franchisees.

We will usually already have seen a copy of the prospectus, the franchise information pack, the franchise agreement, financial projections, and information about the performance of any pilot operations.

We would look to lend these franchisees up to 70% of their total set-up costs. This applies to franchise re-sales, where a franchisee is buying an established franchise unit from an existing franchisor, as well as for a new franchise unit."

What might cause your franchise concept to fail?

Whilst this may seem like a rather pessimistic consideration when you are planning a new franchise, it is worthwhile giving the subject due consideration. Not least so that you can identify, and then avoid, potential pitfalls.

Bill Hendrie is a Franchise Development Consultant with The Franchise Development Centre. He has long experience working in franchise businesses, and has been a franchise consultant since 2009.

Having supported many franchisors in their journey towards launching their franchise, Bill highlighted the following key issues:

*"The archetypal franchise development mistake is **making the wrong choice of franchisee**. Some franchisors will make mistakes in setting their skill set requirements. Most particularly, it is easy to overlook the need for franchisees to be good sales people. Teaching a franchisee of a drain cleaning franchise how to clean drains is one thing. But it can be very much harder to teach that franchisee how to sell. At the end of the day, all businesses involve an element of selling, whether you call it that or not."*

Bill also says: *"Franchises often run into difficulty because they have **not done enough territory analysis**. The distances that customers may be prepared to travel to get to your franchisee may vary widely from one franchise concept to another. Your franchisees' success or failure will also depend on* demographics pertaining to their part of the country, and again there can be huge differences from one territory to another. It is easy, particularly in the early stages, to grant territories that are too large. The result is either that one franchisee will do exceptionally well, at the cost of other neighbouring franchisees, or otherwise that you lose significant sales opportunities, because the franchisee's territory is too large for them to be able to exploit to best advantage.

Another typical downfall is **launching your franchise too soon**. Generally speaking, you will want your concept to have been trading for at least a year, either directly by you or otherwise through a pilot, before you consider franchising it. Even then, and particularly where your initial success was attributable to your personal skills and abilities, you need time to invest in your business so that there is a sufficient support system in place to ensure that you can steer your franchisees can be as successful as you.

Under-investment. Franchisors are set for failure if they attempt to build their franchise system on a shoe-string. You will need to put money into your concept and - crucially – be prepared to lose it if things don't work out. Your franchise system will need continuing investment, even once you have got franchisees on board. As your business grows, you will need to source manpower and skills, including a marketing team, both internal and external expertise, and all other head office functions.

Your franchisees will want to see **continued value in your system**. They will want to see a continuous process of innovation in new products or new initiatives and ideas. You need to be providing ongoing support, so that your franchisees always perceive that they are better off in your system than outside it. If your franchisee support effectively stops once the franchisee has finished his/her *training and got their operations manual, the franchisee will not stick it out. They will eventually under-perform and/or drift out of your franchise."*

The future of franchising

Clive Sawyer is Managing Director of **Business Options**, a specialist franchise and business expansion consultancy. Clive regularly speaks on franchising at seminars, exhibitions and also runs British Franchise Association workshops for prospective and existing franchisors. Clive has also written 3 books on franchising.

Clive believes that franchising's place as a current and attractive way for businesses to expand in the UK is only going to increase over the next twenty years. But he also argues that the way franchisors operate will need to change to reflect our fast changing business and consumer environment.

"For franchising to remain a credible business expansion model", says Clive, *"it is important that it remains current and reflects the way businesses operate and overall consumer behaviour. When the first Wimpy opened in the UK back in 1954, nobody could have guessed the changes in technology that were to come or the changes in consumer buying behaviour. It is less than 30 years ago that the World Web Web was invented and who would have imagined that currently over 12% of all retail sales in the UK are made online and the UK's average weekly online spending is fast approaching £1 billion. The ways people live their lives and buy services and products has dramatically changed. Just like any other business, for a franchise business to be successful in the*

future, it must ensure that it aligns itself with the changing needs and buying behaviours of its customers."

Clive explains that the fundamentals of franchising still remain as true today as they have done over the last 60 years: *"Your business must be proven and profitable, and you need an operating system which your franchisees follow and which is continually enhanced to ensure that it remains competitive and current."*

"When franchising a business, businesses will still need to invest sufficient time and resource to ensure that their franchise is set-up correctly. Despite more and more information being available online and for free, creating the right franchise model for a business still requires expertise which most business owners will not possess. Most businesses will have had no need to keep abreast of all the developments in franchising, both legally and culturally, and are also unlikely to know the pitfalls and how to avoid them when franchising their business. The old adage "You don't know what you don't know" still remains true, and therefore whatever technological and cultural changes we experience over the next few decades, there will still be a need to use the services of professional franchise experts if a business is to maximise the opportunities and avoid the pitfalls that franchising any business brings."

In the future, believes Clive, there will be changes that franchisors need to adopt and embrace if they are going to be successful: He suggests for key considerations:

> ➢ Speed of response:
> *"We are now in a world where people expect virtually instant access to information and instant responses"* says Clive. *"With the explosion in social media and online chat platforms*

people now are used to and expect instant responses to their questions. Franchisors need to understand that the traditional method of handling prospective franchisee enquiries, whereby people completed application forms, and then a franchise brochure was sent out a couple of days later will no longer be appropriate. Franchisors will have to adapt their approach and provide virtually instantaneous responses to franchise enquiries. Franchisors will also have to provide information and resources to their franchisees so that franchisees can respond very quickly to their customers."

➢ Attention span:
"Recent research has shown that more than half of all smartphone use consisted of short bursts of less than 30 seconds of activity. This means the way franchisors market to prospective franchisees will need to be in smaller chunks; and the way your franchisees market their services to their customers will need to be aligned to this new style of consumer behaviour."

➢ Routes to market:
"Over the last 10 years we have seen a dramatic change in the way people look for information and how they buy. The trend towards online buying will continue and face to face interaction with customers will get less and less. Social media platforms will continue to change as new platforms are created and more established platforms fall out of trend. Therefore the days of following the same franchisor marketing strategy for years will no longer be appropriate. More time, resource and frequency will need to be spent by

franchisors in adapting and changing the way they promote both their franchise opportunity and the services of their franchisees."

➤ Franchisee fees:
"The traditional way franchisors price their franchise and then set their ongoing fee structure will need to change. There may be a shift towards lower upfront fees and, in order to ensure that franchisors have sufficient funds to continually develop and keep pace with the quickly changing marketplace, ongoing franchisees are likely to increase."

➤ Legislation:
Clive forecasts that it is only matter of time before the UK sees the introduction of franchise specific legislation. *"With the growing litigious world we live in, I can see that it will be only a matter of time that UK franchise legislation is introduced. This may be as simple as a formal disclosure requirement or a more complex formal franchisor registration requirement."* Although Clive acknowledges that franchise legislation will place a burden on franchisors and increase the cost of franchising, he believes that better protection for people buying a franchise will be a positive step.

"The inevitable move to a faster changing business and consumer environment should make franchising as a business model even more attractive to prospective franchisees, as it is likely to become harder for small start-up business to invest the money needed to keep up with their fast changing marketplace. The benefits that franchising brings through economies of scale and with the franchisor being responsible for keeping the business competitive

for all their franchisees, may in the future make franchising even more attractive for people who want to have their own business compared with starting a business from scratch."

More details about Clive and Business Options can be found at www.businessoptions.biz.

Appendix A

Operations Manual Outline

Topic	Item
Introduction	About the business
	Ownership of the manual, and intellectual property rights in the manual
	Confidentiality
	Disclaimers
	Franchisor contact details: who to contact, and how
Premises	Guidelines for selection and location of premises
	Recommended/nominated architects/agents
	Fit Out Specifications
	Fixtures and Fittings
	Furniture
	Signage
	Required lease provisions?

Products and Services	Detailed specifications of your products and services
	"Core" (or mandatory) products and/or services that the franchisee must offer
	Discretionary services
	Procedures for providing products and/or services
Pricing	Recommended pricing
Equipment	Equipment to be purchased from Franchisor / nominated supplier
	Equipment to be purchased by the Franchisee
Stock	Stock to be purchased from Franchisor / nominated supplier
	Stock to be purchased by the Franchisee Minimum stock levels
	Ordering procedures
Franchisee start-up procedures	Any licences or regulatory approvals required?
	Setting up a limited company
	VAT registration requirements?
Training	Initial Training Programme for franchisees
	Ongoing training
	Health & safety procedures
Customer service	Process for receiving orders, receiving payments, billing, customer record retention

	Customer feedback process
	Customer complaints procedure
IT	What systems (eg CRM) must the franchisee use?
	IT support
Staff	Recruitment procedures and franchisor approval requirements
	Template terms & conditions
	HR policies and procedures
	Uniforms
	Standards of appearance and behaviour
Accounts and Records	Franchisee bank accounts, standing orders etc
	Fees payable by the franchisee, as per the franchise agreement
	Payment procedure for management service fee and/or any other fees payable to franchisor under the franchise agreement
	Reporting procedures, use of CRM or other systems
	Records management
Business Planning	Responsibility for franchisee business plan
	Franchisor approvals required
Marketing and advertising	Franchisee local marketing

	Franchisee participation in national marketing initiatives
	Use of social media
	Franchisor approvals required

Appendix B

DATED   2016

(1) [Franchise] Limited

(2) [   ] LIMITED ("Franchisee")

(3) [   ] ("Principal")

"[NAME OF FRANCHISE]"
FRANCHISE AGREEMENT

NB1: Note that this document is a very generalised description of a typical format of Franchise Agreement. It is for information only, and should not be used or modified without professional legal advice.

NB2: Note that there is no such thing as a "standard" form of franchise agreement that works for everyone. Every business is different, and the form and content of your franchise agreement must reflect in detail the way that the franchisor does business, and the standards that they expect from their franchisees. For franchisors, if your franchise agreement is not "tailor made" for your business, it will never protect you properly.

[Name of Franchisee]
[Territory]

(FOR LIMITED COMPANY FRANCHISEE)

GOLDSTEIN LEGAL

11 High Street Windsor Berkshire SL4 1LD

tel: 01753 865165

email: info@goldsteinlegal.co.uk

www.goldsteinlegal.co.uk

© Goldstein Legal 2016

This Agreement is dated ....

(1) [FRANCHISE ENTITY] LIMITED a company incorporated in England and Wales under company number .... and having its registered office at .... ("the Franchisor");

(2) [   ] LIMITED a company incorporated in [England and Wales] under company number [   ]   and   having its registered office at [   ]   ("the Franchisee"); and

(3) [   ] of [   ] ("the Principal")

Recitals

A. The Franchisor, as a result of considerable time and effort and investment and practical business experience, has developed the [Franchise] Business.

B. The Franchisor has built up a substantial reputation and goodwill in the Trade Mark, which is associated with the highest standards of products and services.

C. The Franchisor is the owner of the Intellectual Property (or is licensed by the owner to use the Intellectual Property in the manner envisaged in this agreement).

D. The Franchisee wishes to acquire from the Franchisor the right and franchise to operate a [Name of Franchise] Business in the Territory and the Franchisor has agreed to grant to the Franchisee the right to operate a [Name of Franchise] Business in accordance with the terms of this agreement.

Now it is agreed as follows:

1. Interpretation
   1.1 In this agreement the following words and or expressions shall have the meanings set out below:-

"Business"   [add details]

["Database"   the customer database owned by the Franchisor for the purposes of the [Name of Franchise] Business]

"Equipment"   such equipment, stationery and materials, including the items [included in the Start-Up Package], and such other equipment stationery and materials [including software and uniforms] as is specified in the Operations Manual from time to time

"Gross Revenues"	[add details]
"[Name of Franchise] Business"	the business of providing the [Products and Services] using the Intellectual Property
"[Name of Franchise] Network"	the network of businesses providing [Products and Services] under the Trade Mark
["Current Image"	the internal and external physical appearance of Stores including without limitation as it relates to signage, fascia, colour schemes, menu boards, lighting, furniture, finishes, décor, materials and equipment as may reasonably be changed from time to time by the Franchisor]
"Incapacity"	the Principal's inability through physical or mental cause to perform their duties under this agreement
"Initial Fee"	the fee specified in clause 4.1.1
"Initial Training"	the training provided by the Franchisor to the Franchisee in the correct operation of the System as specified by the Franchisor and as referred to in clause 6 below
"Intellectual Property"	[add details]
"Key Person"	the person named in Schedule 1 or such other person as the Franchisor may (in its absolute discretion) approve from time to time

"Minimum Performance Criteria"	the criteria referred to in clause 8.7.1 below
"Month"	a calendar month or such other 12 periods in each calendar year as the Franchisor shall stipulate
"National Accounts"	those clients either gained as a result of approaches by the Franchisor or identified by the Franchisor and/or specified as such in the Operations Manual from time to time
"New Franchise Agreement"	the latest edition of the Franchisor's standard form of franchise agreement then being offered to its franchisees which may contain terms materially different from the terms of this agreement
"Operations Manual"	a manual or manuals setting out the operations and procedures for running a [Name of Franchise] Business as may be updated by the Franchisor from time to time
"Products"	................, as more particularly described in the Operations Manual
["Purchase Option"	the option granted pursuant to clause 17.1 and Schedule 2 for the Franchisor to purchase the Business from the Franchisee]
"Services"	......................., as more particularly described in the Operations Manual
["Start-Up Package"	the items listed in the table in Schedule 1] OR [Equipment List]

["Store/Premises"	[retail] premises at which the Business is operated under the terms of this agreement]
"System"	all of the following which are more particularly described in the Operations Manual: (a) the substantial know-how and expertise developed by the Franchisor in the provision of [Products and Services] and (b) the service format and standards of quality offered by a [Name of Franchise] Business [including proprietary designs and colour schemes for restaurant buildings, equipment, layout and décor, proprietary menu and food preparation and service formats, uniform product and quality specifications]
"Term"	a period of 3 years commencing on the date of this agreement
"Territory"	the area described in Schedule 1
"Trade Mark"	the mark or marks referred to in Schedule 1 and such other unregistered and or registered trade marks, trade names or service marks in addition to or in substitution of any of them as may be specified by the Franchisor from time to time
"Vehicle"	....
"Website"	the website operated by the Franchisor for the operation of the System
["Week"	each period of 7 days ending on a [Saturday]]
["Year"	a 12 month period commencing on the date of this Agreement or any anniversary thereof]

1.2 Subject to clause 26.9 any reference in this agreement to writing includes fax transmission and email or similar means of communication.

1.3 Any reference in this agreement to any provision of a statute or statutory instrument shall be construed as a reference to that provision as amended, re-enacted or extended.

1.4 Any reference in this agreement to a person includes natural persons and partnerships, firms and other such unincorporated bodies, corporate bodies and all other legal persons of whatever kind and however constituted.

1.5 The headings in this agreement are for convenience only and shall not affect its interpretation.

1.6 If there are two or more persons as Principal under this agreement, all covenants and agreements on the part of the Principal shall be deemed to be joint and several covenants and agreements on their part.

1.7 Any reference to one gender includes all other genders and the singular includes the plural and vice versa.

1.8 References to clauses or schedules are to clauses or schedules to this agreement and Schedules are deemed to be incorporated in this agreement and references to this agreement shall include Schedules.

2. Grant of Rights

2.1 The Franchisor grants the Franchisee the [non-exclusive] right to operate the Business within the Territory for the Term subject to the terms and conditions of this agreement.

[add terms relating to exclusivity, right for franchisor to sell in Territory, right for franchisee to sell outside the Territory etc]

3. Term and Renewal

3.1 This agreement shall, subject to the provisions for prior termination as set out in this agreement, subsist for the Term.

[add renewal rights, if any]

4. Fees, Payments and Commissions

4.1 In consideration of the grant of the right and licence to operate a [Name of Franchise] Business the Franchisee shall pay without any deduction or set-off:-

4.1.1 the Initial Fee of £.......... and the Franchisor acknowledges it has already received £_____ by way of deposit from the Franchisee which shall be credited towards the Initial Fee payable on the date of this Agreement

[add details of Management Service Fee, Advertising Levy (if any), Training Fee (if any), and payment terms]

5. Franchisor's Initial Obligations

The Franchisor will provide or make available to the Franchisee the following:

[add details]

6. Training

[add details of Initial Training and any further training that the Franchisor may require]

7. Franchisor's Continuing Obligations

The Franchisor shall:

7.1 provide the Franchisee with know-how, advice and guidance relating to the Business, including on-site liaison at such intervals and times as the Franchisor shall determine. *[add further details as appropriate]*

8. Franchisee's Obligations

[This section tends to be the longest part of the agreement, setting out in detail how the Franchisee is expected to operate the franchise. This needs to be drafted bespoke for each client, as no two franchise operations are ever the same]

The Franchisee shall:- *[add details]*

8.1 Starting Up

8.2 Carrying on the Business

8.3 Stores/Premises

8.4 Products

8.5 Services

8.6 Vehicle

8.7 Customers

8.8 Premises

8.9 Staff

8.10 Quality Standards

8.9 Minimum Performance Criteria

8.9.1 The Franchisee is required to achieve .... ("the Minimum Performance Criteria").

[add detail of consequences of failure to achieve]
8.10 Communications

[Add details of ownership of telephone numbers, email addresses, domain names etc, and procedures on termination of the franchise]

8.11   Business Plan

[add details]

9. Advertising

9.1 The Franchisee shall *[add details]*. All advertising, marketing or promotions by the Franchisee must be approved in advance by the Franchisor and must display the Trade Mark in the manner stipulated by the Franchisor.

10. Aooounting Records

10.1 The Franchisee shall: *[add details]*

11. Status of Franchisee and Principal

[add details]

12. Insurance

[add details]

13. Trade Mark

[add details]

14. Sale of Business

[add details]

15. Non-Competition and Confidentiality

[add details]

16. Death or Incapacity of Principal

16.1 If the Principal (or in the case of joint Principals the last surviving Principal) shall die during the Term:-

[add details]

16.4 In the event of the Incapacity of the Principal (or in the case of joint Principals, of both Principals) lasting for a continuous period of [.............], the Franchisor may by written notice *[add details]*

17. Termination

17.1 The Franchisor may, without prejudice to any other rights or remedies available to it, terminate this agreement immediately by written notice to the Franchisee, upon a material breach of this agreement, and any of the following shall be deemed to be a material breach but the list shall not be deemed to be exhaustive, and upon such termination all rights of the Franchisee under this agreement shall cease: *[add details]*

[17.2 This Agreement shall automatically terminate without notice being given to the franchisee if the Franchisee ceases to be registered for VAT, whereupon the Franchisor shall be entitled to claim damages as if such termination had occurred because of the Franchisee's breach of this Agreement.]

18 Consequences of Termination

18.1 Upon termination for any cause, the Franchisee shall immediately: *[add details]*

19. Post Termination Restrictions

[add details]

20. Representations

[add dotails]

21. Guarantee and Obligations of the Principal

[add details]

22. Indemnity

[add details]

23. Improvements

23.1 The Franchisee shall, when required by the Franchisor in writing, introduce any improvement, modifications or change to the System and the Business in the manner specified by the Franchisor *[add details]*.

23.2 In order that the Franchisee, the Franchisor and its other franchisees may all benefit from the free interchange of ideas the Franchisee shall permit the Franchisor to introduce into the

System and/or the Operations Manual any improvements which it may have notified to the Franchisor without payment being made for it and shall enter into a royalty free exclusive licence with the Franchisor in a form agreed for this purpose.

24. Operations Manual

24.1 The Operations Manual shall form part of this agreement and in the event of any conflict between the provisions of the Operations Manual and this agreement, this agreement shall prevail.

24.2 The copyright and all other rights in the text of the Operations Manual, the Franchisor's website and other documents supplied to the Franchisee are secret and confidential and vest solely in the Franchisor.

24.3 The Franchisee and the Principal each acknowledge that all goodwill associated with or arising from the use of the Intellectual Property shall belong to the Franchisor and that the Franchisee only has the right to benefit from such goodwill to the extent provided for in this agreement.

24.4 Where in this agreement there is a reference to a requirement of the Franchisor it shall be deemed to include any requirement contained in the Operations Manual.

25. Data Protection

[add details]

26. General

26.1 Nothing in this agreement shall be construed as making the parties partners or joint venturers nor render any party liable for any of the debts or obligations of any other party. Neither the Franchisee nor the Principal is, nor shall either hold itself out nor permit others to hold it out as the agent, director or employee of the Franchisor and under no circumstances shall the Franchisee or the Principal have authority to bind the Franchisor nor hold itself out to any third party as having such authority.

26.2 This Agreement shall be suspended for any period during which either party reasonably believes that the other is prevented or hindered from complying with any of their obligations under it by any cause beyond its reasonable control as the case may be, including but not restricted to strikes, fuel shortages, war, civil disorder and natural disasters. If such period of suspension exceeds 180 days, then either party may upon giving written notice to the other require that the agreement be terminated whereupon all money due to the Franchisor shall be paid immediately.

[add any additional "boilerplate" clauses, as appropriate]
26.10 Save as expressly provided for in this agreement, no term of this agreement shall be enforceable under the Contracts (Rights of Third Parties) Act 1999 by a third party.

26.12 The Franchisor may assign or otherwise deal with the benefit and burden of the whole or any part of this agreement without consent from the Franchisee, and in the case of an assignment, if it procures that the assignee enters into a direct covenant with the Franchisee to observe and perform all the Franchisor's obligations in this agreement the Franchisor shall be released and discharged from all obligations hereunder.

27. National Accounts

[add details, if appropriate]

28. Jurisdiction

This agreement is governed by and construed in accordance with the laws of England and Wales and the parties submit to the exclusive jurisdiction of the English courts.

27. Alternative Dispute Resolution

[add details]

Schedule 1

[add details]

[Start-Up Package/Equipment List]:

Key Person:

Minimum percentage of shares to be held by Principal:

Territory:

Trade Mark:

Schedule 2

The Purchase Option *[add details if appropriate]*

LEGAL ADVICE – IMPORTANT

The Franchisee and the Principal each represent to the Franchisor that they have reviewed this agreement with the benefit of having taken independent legal advice and understand and accept the terms and conditions of this agreement

Signed by xxxxxxxxxxxxxx	date......................
Signed by .... **NAME** On behalf of **[Franchisee]** in the presence of: Witness: .... (signature) Name: .... Address: .... Occupation:	date......................

Signed by	
.... **NAME** **Principal** in the presence of: Witness: .... (signature) Name: .... Address: .... Occupation:	date.........................

Index

A

Accounting Records 89, 166
Advertising 12, 79, 88, 118, 119, 120, 154, 163, 166
Agency 30, 31, 127

B

balance sheet 27, 49, 51, 100
bfa 1, 32, 33, 34, 41, 78, 85, 86, 87, 89, 125, 137, 138, 139, 140, 141
Brand licensing 28
British Franchise Association 32, 33, 77, 85, 125, 137, 147
"business format" franchise 4
business planning 16, 136, 154

C

cash flow 49, 55, 100
cash-flow 27, 43
Code of Ethics 33, 41, 137, 138
competition 58, 76, 80, 125, 167
Confidential Information 64, 115
confidentiality agreement 84, 86, 116
consultant 32, 33, 34, 76, 92, 93, 141, 144
Copyright 63, 100, 101, 169
CRM 6, 9, 37, 48, 63, 154

D

Database rights 63
deposit agreement 84, 86
Deposit agreement 86
Design rights 64
Discovery Days 122, 128
Distribution 30
domain names 21, 60, 88, 165

E

F

H

I

Public Relations 127

Q

QC 48, 99, 128, 139, 165
Quality Control 48

R

Risk Factors 58
royalties 5, 78

S

social media 88, 100, 118, 119, 122, 123, 124, 127, 139, 148, 149,
          155
Start-Up Pack 49, 72, 73, 77, 158, 160, 172

T

Territory Mapping 65, 131, 132, 133, 135, 136
Territory Plan 65, 66
The Legal Pack 84
Trade Marks 4, 21, 28, 46, 60, 61, 62, 63, 89, 157, 159, 161, 166, 172
training 1, 4, 8, 18, 20, 29, 41, 45, 46, 47, 55, 63, 65, 67, 68, 72, 74,
          77, 82, 87, 88, 95, 96, 97, 98, 99, 100, 101, 139, 140, 146,
          153, 159, 163, 164
Training Programme 4, 20, 67, 95, 96, 97, 98, 100, 139, 153

U

Under-capitalisation 44

W

website 9, 16, 32, 48, 63, 77, 85, 119, 120, 122, 123, 124, 128, 138,
          139, 161, 169
Website marketing 120, 122, 124

Lightning Source UK Ltd.
Milton Keynes UK
UKRC02n0927180318
319614UK00001B/3